COLLINS *rambler's guide*

north wales

D0550504

The Ramblers

HARVEY

richard sale
photographs by tony oliver

HarperCollins*Publishers*
77–85 Fulham Palace Road
London W6 8JB

The HarperCollins website address is: www.**fire**and**water**.com

05 04 03 02 01

10 9 8 7 6 5 4 3 2

First published 2000

Series Editor Richard Sale
© in this edition HarperCollins*Publishers* Ltd.
© in the text Richard Sale
© in the photographs Tony Oliver
© in the maps Harvey Map Services Ltd., Doune, Perthshire
Walk profiles by Carte Blanche

We are grateful to the following members of the Ramblers' Association who kindly assisted in checking the walks in this book: Syd Caplan, John Carson, Geoff Elliott, Neville Fernley, Monica and Denis McAteer, Tom Morris, Bob Smith, Doug Whitehouse, Ron Williams and Colin Yarwood.

The profiles given for each walk give an indication of the steepness and number of climbs on the route. The times on the profiles are calculated according to the Naismith formula which suggests one hour for each five map kilometres (three map miles) covered, together with an additional 30 minutes for each 300m (1,000ft) of ascent. For most walkers the formula underestimates the time taken for several reasons. Firstly few walkers complete a walk as a route march; secondly, there is no allowance for the terrain crossed, and it is easier to walk quickly over short grass than rough moor; thirdly, there is no allowance for stopping to admire the view, places of interest etc; and finally there is no allowance for rest stops. Rest stops tend to become both longer and more frequent as the walk length increases, so the time error increases as walks get longer. Please check yourself against the times on the first walks you attempt to gauge the time you will take on others.

ISBN 0 00 220113 5

Designed and produced by Drum Enterprises Ltd.
Printed and bound in Great Britain by Scotprint, Musselburgh

CONTENTS

How to use this book

This book contains route maps and descriptions for 30 walks. Each walk is graded (see p.3) and areas of interest are indicated by symbols (see below). For each walk particular points of interest are denoted by a capital letter both in the text and on the map (where the letter appears in a red box). In the text the route descriptions are prefixed by lower-case letters. We recommend that you read the whole description, including the tinted box at the start of each walk, before setting out.

Key to maps

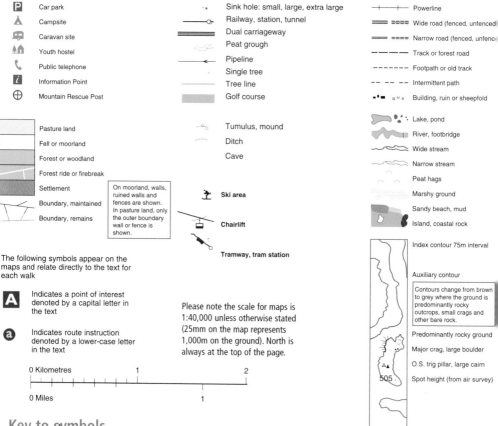

P	Car park	
▲	Campsite	
🚐	Caravan site	
🏠	Youth hostel	
☏	Public telephone	
i	Information Point	
⊕	Mountain Rescue Post	

	Pasture land
	Fell or moorland
	Forest or woodland
	Forest ride or firebreak
	Settlement
	Boundary, maintained
	Boundary, remains

On moorland, walls, ruined walls and fences are shown. In pasture land, only the outer boundary wall or fence is shown.

Sink hole: small, large, extra large
Railway, station, tunnel
Dual carriageway
Peat grough
Pipeline
Single tree
Tree line
Golf course

Tumulus, mound
Ditch
Cave

🎿 Ski area

🚡 Chairlift

Tramway, tram station

Powerline
Wide road (fenced, unfenced)
Narrow road (fenced, unfenced)
Track or forest road
Footpath or old track
Intermittent path
Building, ruin or sheepfold

Lake, pond
River, footbridge
Wide stream
Narrow stream
Peat hags
Marshy ground
Sandy beach, mud
Island, coastal rock

Index contour 75m interval

Auxiliary contour

Contours change from brown to grey where the ground is predominantly rocky outcrops, small crags and other bare rock.

Predominantly rocky ground

Major crag, large boulder

O.S. trig pillar, large cairn

505 Spot height (from air survey)

The following symbols appear on the maps and relate directly to the text for each walk

A Indicates a point of interest denoted by a capital letter in the text

a Indicates route instruction denoted by a lower-case letter in the text

Please note the scale for maps is 1:40,000 unless otherwise stated (25mm on the map represents 1,000m on the ground). North is always at the top of the page.

0 Kilometres   1   2

0 Miles   1

Key to symbols

The walks in this book are graded from 1–5 according to the level of difficulty, with 1 being the easiest and 5 the most difficult. We recommend that walks graded 4 or higher (or grade 3 where indicated) should only be undertaken by experienced walkers who are competent in the use of map and compass and who are aware of the difficulties of the terrain they will encounter. The use of detailed maps is recommended for all routes.

At the start of each walk there is a series of symbols that indicate particular areas of interest associated with the route.

 Birdlife

 Good views

 Other wildlife

 Historical interest

 Wild flowers

 Woodland

INTRODUCTION

For those who love the hills, who delight in their wildness and rugged beauty, whose spirits rise as they journey closer to landscapes where the horizon is tilted beyond the norm, there will always be one range, above others, that is pre-eminent – the range that first grabbed the imagination and held it firm. For me those hills are the mountains of Snowdonia: the sharp, angular peaks of Snowdon and the Glyders; the whaleback ridges of the Carneddau; the awkward, uncompromising Rhinogs; the vast faces and lovely cwms of Cadair Idris.

This book explores those landscapes, and others besides, seeking out not only the scenery that makes Snowdonia special, but the history, folklore and natural history which make it unique.

SNOWDONIA

In 1951 Snowdonia was the third of Britain's National Parks (after the Peak and Lake District Parks) to be designated. It is a large Park, second in size only to the Lake District and, at almost 840 sq. miles (2,175km²), covering more than 10 per cent of Wales. Wales has two other National Parks (the Brecon Beacons and Pembrokeshire Coast), but Snowdonia is the most distinctly Welsh. Not in its landscape of course (how could that be?), but in its feel. The overwhelming majority of the Park's inhabitants speak Welsh as a first language, as do an equally large percentage of those who live in the immediately surrounding area. The language is a cultural

Y Garn and Foel Goch from Llyn Ogwen

heritage, one which has allowed the folklore of Celtic Britain to survive in a way that few other areas of Britain can claim. Virtually every feature of the landscape, even the bumps and notches of the highest peaks has a name, one linked to an old myth or legend. And those legends live on rather than having been lost as the Celts were replaced by the Romans, who were then ousted by the Saxons, and so on, as happened in England.

It might be argued (and often is in certain quarters) that the name Snowdonia is an offense to this Welsh heritage. The park should, the argument goes, be replaced by the Welsh name for the area – Eryri. But Snowdonia is itself an ancient name: Llywelyn ap Iorwerth, Prince of Gwynedd, known as Llywelyn Fawr (Llywelyn the Great) was calling himself Dominus Snaudoniae, Lord of Snowdonia, in the first years of the 13th century, though the derivation of the name is not well understood. Why should Snowdon have been called by that name when there are many other mountains in Britain more deserving of being the Snow Peak: it is conjectured that sailors on trading ships to and from Ireland gave the peak the name as they used it as a landmark on their crossing of the Celtic Sea.

Eryri is a beautiful name, but its meaning is as disputed as the origins of Snowdon. Most works translate it as Land of Eagles, and eryr does indeed mean eagle in Welsh. But the Welsh for snow is eira so perhaps the Welsh name also meant 'snow peaks' and was translated into English. To add, rather than clear, the confusion, there are those who claim the name derives from a Welsh rendering of the Latin *oriri*, meaning 'to rise' when applied to a landscape. Then Eryri would mean Land of Mountains.

Yr Wyddfa

THE WALKS

Mist-filled Nantgwynant

The walks have been chosen to explore all the main mountain groups which make up Snowdonia. Many, as would be expected, visit the high peaks. But the National Park covers a diverse range of scenery, and some of the walks are lowland, chosen to explore valleys or gorges. All have been chosen to do justice not only to the area's scenic beauty, but to the other aspects which make Snowdonia such a rich landscape.

There are, too, a small number of walks just outside the National Park: Snowdonia has one of the highest rainfalls of any area in Britain (around 100in/2,500mm annually) and walkers will have days when the high peaks are shrouded in cloud and too wet for all but the positively certifiable. On those days the 'rain shadow' regions to the west (the Lleyn Peninsula), north (Anglesey) and east (the Berwyns) frequently offer dry alternatives, and a route is offered in each.

Tal-y-Llyn from Cwm Cau

The walks are circular with two exceptions. The first is the Nantlle Ridge, where to have tried to construct a circular walk would have been to destroy its character; the second is the traverse of Snowdon (Walk 2). In each case the public transport option for a return is given (though in the case of the Snowdon traverse a circular option is also offered). For the Nantlle Ridge the bus option involves a trip into, and out of, Caernarfon which seems involved and tedious, but actually means a total journey of little more than 20 miles (32km).

For each walk an approximate time is given. These are based on the well-known 'Naismith Formula' which allows one hour for each 5 map-kilometres (3 map-miles) plus an extra half-hour for each 300m (1,000ft) of ascent. These strictures have been modified to allow for the terrain covered by each walk: it is quicker to travel a few hundred yards along the Miners' Track then across the heather moorland of the northern Rhinogs. It also takes less energy and here the major problem with Naismith is revealed. The formula assumes an unladen walker of limitless energy who wastes no time admiring the view. Real walkers, as opposed to Naismith automatons, take rests (which are both more frequent and last longer as they become tired) and stop for the view, or the wildlife, or any of another dozen or more reasons. Please use the times as a guide only, modifying them according to your personal characteristics after completing a couple of routes.

The majority of the walks follow distinct paths. Please keep to them in order to avoid unnecessary erosion of other sections of the hillside. Please, also, be sympathetic to any sections of constructed path (or path under construction) you encounter. It would obviously be better if there were no such paths, better still if there were no scarring pathlines across the popular hills. But the only way to achieve that would be to ban walkers.

Most of the routes follow public rights of way, but some also follow permissive (or courtesy) paths. On all the routes the walker should remember that he/she is crossing private land. Much of it is farmland, usually used for sheep grazing – please keep dogs under close control.

On the permissive paths it is also important that walkers remember that at any time permission to walk could be rescinded: the attitude of the landowners to the walkers behind you will be influenced by your behaviour.

Finally, no grading system is implied by the ordering of the walks in the book. It just starts with the highest peak, Snowdon, moves east across the highest ranges, then heads south and ends with the outlying areas. The grade according to difficultly is indicated at the beginning of each walk (see How to use this book, p.4)

Looking from Waun Oer towards Cadair Idris

THE WELSH LANGUAGE

An understanding of the basics of the Welsh language will be of help to all walkers, allowing the landscape to come alive.

Welsh has its roots, as one would expect, in the Celtic languages of continental Europe and so shares a common ancestry with the Teutonic-based English language, though there is little obvious similarity now, many centuries after the split. The Celtic language that crossed from the continent was itself subject to a split, the Goidelic form occurring in Ireland, the Isle of Man and Scotland, while the Brythonic form dominated the rest of Britain, yielding the Welsh and Cornish languages. The Breton language of French Brittany is also a Brythonic language. To differentiate between the Goidelic (Gaelic) and Brythonic languages the former is called Q Celtic, the latter P Celtic, the reason being the pronunciation of 'qu'. Q Celtic pronounces this as 'qu' (or, rather 'c'), while P Celtic pronounces it 'p'. Thus, in mountain terms, Welsh has 'pen' while Gaelic has 'ceann',

To the English eye the Welsh language is an unreadable mass of vowel-less words with consonants back-to-back. This is, of course, not so, but based on the misconception that the alphabets of the two languages are the same. In fact Welsh has extra consonants, dd, ll and ff being letters – not as strange as it seems, for remember that English has w, ie. uu – and can utilise w and y as vowels. While dd and ll have their own sounds – the former as 'th' (as in 'then'); the latter as 'thl' – ff is pronounced f, the Welsh f being pronounced v. Thus Tryfan is pronounced 'Try-vane'. Also cwm (mountain hollow) is acceptable, and pronounced coom.

A second, and radical, departure from English is initial mutation, the alteration of the initial consonants of words when the final sound of the preceding word is of particular form. The reason for this appears to be straightforwardly aesthetic. However the (apparently random) interchangeability of, say, fawr and mawr (large) or fach and bach (small), not to mention other worse forms, eg. cam – gam – ngham – cham, makes the casual observer wince.

Despite this explanation, however, the English visitor on his first trip to Wales will sympathise with Nathaniel Hawthorne, the 19th-century American writer. He visited Bangor and wrote: 'At Bangor we … hired a carriage and two horses for some Welsh place, the name of which I forget; neither can I remember a single name of any of the places through which

Cwm Cau, Cadair Idris

we posted on that day, nor could I spell them if I heard them pronounced, nor pronounce them if I saw them spelt'.

The visitor has less trouble with Welsh personal names, Christian or surnames. Indeed the lack of trouble seems to be the fact that there appear to be only half-a-dozen surnames in the whole of Wales. The story immediately comes to mind of the Welsh male voice choir refused entry to an East European country because the frontier guard would not believe that there was not a decadent western plot behind a large group of men, ninety per cent of whom were called Davies.

Originally the Welsh used the patronymic form of name, that is a child had its own first name, then added 'ap XX', meaning child of XX. But, it is said, many years ago an English judge touring Wales became so appalled by the stream of plaintiffs and defendants with names such as Rhys ap Llywelyn, Taliesin ap Iorwerth and worse, that he decreed that the naming system should be rationalised:

> Take ten, he said, and call them Rice
> Take another ten and called them Price
> Now Roberts name some hundred score
> And Williams name a legion more
> And call, he moaned in languid tones,
> Call the other thousands – Jones

To attempt a comprehensive glossary of useful Welsh names would be doomed to failure, but listed below are those that will allow the first visitor to understand the area he or she is traversing a little better.

Aber – confluence, but usually a river mouth
Afon – river
Allt – hill, especially if wooded
Bach, Fach, Bychan – small
Ban – peak or horn
Bedd – grave
Blaen – head of valley
Bont – bridge
Bwlch – pass
Cadair – chair
Capel – chapel
Carreg – stone
Cefn – ridge
Coch – red
Coed – wood
Craig – crag
Cwm – mountain hollow, a valley with a backslope, as in the famous usage in Western Cwm below Everest
Dinas – town or hillfort
Du, Ddu – black
Dwr – water
Dyffryn – valley
Eglwys – church
Esgair – long ridge
Ffordd – road, pathway
Ffynnon – well, spring
Glas, Las – blue-green
Gors – bog
Gwyn – white
Gwynt – wind
Hafod – summer dwelling, hill-side house for summer use
Hen – old
Hendre – winter dwelling, valley house for winter use
Hir – long
Isaf – lowest
Llech – flat stone
Llwyd – grey
Llyn – lake
Maen – stone (Maen Hir – long stone or standing stone, ie. menhir)
Moel, Foel – bare hill
Mynydd, Fynydd – mountain

Nant – stream, brook
Ogof – cave
Pant – small hollow
Pen – peak
Pistyll – waterfall, usually a water spout
Plas – mansion
Porth – gate
Pwll – pool
Rhaeadr – waterfall
Sarn – causeway
Tref – town
Ty – house
Uchaf – highest
Waun – moor
Ynys – island
Llwybr Cyhoeddus – public footpath
Diolch – thank you

And remember, Dynion is for men, Merched is for ladies.

The Cannon, Tryfan

TRANSPORT

As with all of Britain's country areas, the communities of Snowdonia are not well served by public transport. For each walk the public transport options, where they exist, are given. In one respect Snowdonia's walkers are lucky, the Snowdon Sherpa buses following the major roads through the northern park (linking Bethesda, the Ogwen Valley, Capel Curig, Betws-y-Coed and Llanrwst; Beddgelert and Caernarfon, via Rhyd-Ddu and the Snowdon Ranger; and Llanberis and Beddgelert or Betws-y-Coed via Pen-y-Pass). The Snowdon Sherpa therefore serves many of the starting points for routes in this book and it, as well as the other available services, including the train line along the Conwy Valley to Blaenau Ffestiniog, should be used wherever possible. As anyone who has visited Snowdonia on Bank Holiday weekends knows, the traffic has the potential to spoil a wonderful day.

Gwynedd County Council produces regular timetables for the bus and rail services covering the National Park, and there are dove-tailing timetables for the Conwy area, for Anglesey and for the counties of Powys and Clwyd. Bus and trains timetables can be obtained from Bws Gwynedd on 01286 679535, and (for trains) on 0845 748 4950.

WEATHER

Snowdonia is one of the wettest areas in Britain: the National Park has an average of 100in (2,500mm) of rain annually, while the immediate area of Snowdon has an average of 160in (4,000mm).

As the National Park is also close to the sea, the temperature decrease with altitude is more marked than in other mountain areas. Normally this drop is about 2°F for every 500ft of height gain (about 1°C/150m), but on Snowdon the drop can be as high as 2°F/300ft (1°C/100m). This means that the temperature on the summit of Yr Wyddfa could be 15°F (8°C) lower than that at Pen-y-Pass. Higher differences are common, it being quite often as much as 21°F (12°C) lower on the summit than on the pass.

The prevailing south-westerly wind crosses the Irish Sea and, as a consequence, has lost little of its energy (or apparent enthusiasm) before it hits Snowdonia. The resulting wind chill can drop the apparent temperature still further. There is no simple formula for the calculation of wind chill but as an example, a 15 mph (25km/h) wind would reduce an air temperature of 18°F (10°C) to an apparent temperature of about 4°F (2°C). This is worth remembering because it means that if you are basking in a temperature of about 20°C (68°F), the temperature 'felt' by bare skin on Snowdon's summit in a fresh wind would be only just above freezing.

A local weather forecast is posted at the Gorphywsfa café (usually known as the Pen-y-Pass Café) each day, and also at a number of outdoor gear shops. One can be obtained for the whole National Park by telephoning 0891 500449.

MOUNTAIN RESCUE

Hopefully you will never need the services of Snowdonia's mountain rescue teams, but if there is a problem dial 999 and ask for the police or mountain rescue, ensuring that you know the number of people involved in, and the six figure grid reference of, the incident.

Devil's Kitchen

THE SNOWDON HORSESHOE

A difficult, but rewarding, walk involving some scrambling. A head for heights is absolutely essential, particularly on the ascent of Crib Goch and the traverse of the Pinnacles. A slip on these sections could be fatal. The descent from Snowdon's summit to Bwlch y Saethau is over loose scree made more difficult by the passage of time and countless boots. But the breathtaking views are worth all the effort.

START/FINISH:
The best start is the Pen-y-Pass car park (648 556). Those parking here will find the charge to be almost as steep as the ascent of Crib Goch. Better is to park in Nant Peris (607 582) and to take the Snowdon Sherpa to Pen-y-Pass

DISTANCE/ASCENT:
7½ miles (12km)/3,300ft (1,000m)

APPROXIMATE TIME:
5–6 hours

HIGHEST POINT:
3,560ft (1,085m) Snowdon (Yr Wyddfa) summit

MAPS:
Harveys Snowdonia West; OS Landranger Sheet 115, OS Outdoor Leisure Sheet 17

REFRESHMENTS:
The Gorphwysfa cafe, in the car park, offers everything from snacks to more solid food for the returning walker. There is also a cafe at the summit of Snowdon

ADVICE:
Sections of loose scree, sections of steep scrambling and sections of exposed ridge. Paths well defined except on ascent of Crib Goch where the easiest line is vague

A walker looks out across Nantgwynant from the summit of Y Lliwedd

A   Pen-y-Pass 647 556

Before the road was laid through the Llanberis Pass in the early years of the 19th century, Pen-y-Pass had to be reached on foot. With the wide valley stretched out below uncontaminated by tarmac it must have been an impressive place. It certainly impressed one visitor: 'A perpetual unbroken sabbath stillness reigns through the vast profound, except that at intervals, the piercing cry of the kite or the minstrelsy of the stream is heard'. This comment seems almost religious: in complete contrast someone else noted that the area was 'irregular and rough and full of quagmires'.

Heading towards the Pinnacles from Crib Goch, with Yr Wyddfa behind and Crib-y-ddisgl to the right

The first hotel, fitted neatly into a sheltered cleft in the rock, followed shortly after completion of the road. In the early years of this century a larger hotel, the Gorphwysfa, replaced the earliest, its tenant Owen Rawson Owen staying until his death in 1962. He is remembered, as is his most famous early guest, Geoffrey Winthrop Young, on slate tablets near the door of what is now a youth hostel. The cafe across from the old hotel is a recent addition to the scene.

a   From the car-park the obvious exit is the Miners' Track . Our walk leaves by an exit in the car-park's right wall, taking a path that goes behind the cafe, and heads towards the Llanberis Pass. This is the Pig Track and it is followed straightforwardly as it climbs diagonally across the mountain to reach the obvious pass of Bwlch Moch.

B   The Pig Track

Much ink has been used in the discussion of the derivation of the name Pig. Some say Pig because it reaches Bwlch Moch, the Pass of the Pig, but moch could be from quick not pig, denoting a quick way into Cwm Dyli. Pig does not, in fact, need an explanation say others: since pig is Welsh for peak, it is the Path to the Peak – but where does that leave us with moch? Pig and moch seem too similar to be unattached. The idea that the name is actually Pyg not Pig, from Pen-y-Gwryd, the hotel beyond Pen-y-Pass, is unlikely as the name almost certainly pre-dates the hotel.

b   Ahead now are two paths, the left one being a continuation of the Pig Track that avoids the high ridge en route to Snowdon's summit. Our path is the slab-marked right-hand one that rises deceptively slowly at first, but then rears up to present a real challenge. There is a path of sorts marked out by the passage of boots so that it has become clean and slightly lighter than the surrounding grey rock, but

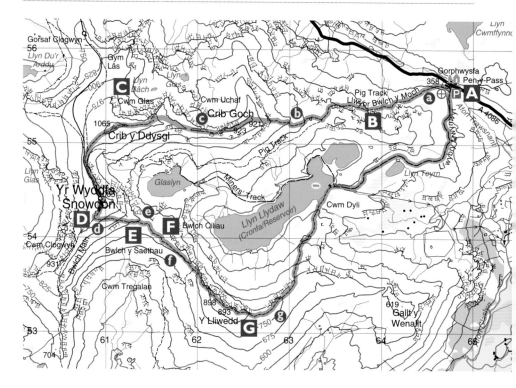

the walker can also pick his own way. The last few feet to the summit of Crib Goch are steep and exposed. The summit is also exposed, but offers outstanding views into the Llanberis Pass, Cwm Glas and into the great hollow that the Horseshoe defines.

C   Cwm Glas 615 555

Cwm is the Welsh word for a mountain hollow. Usually these have been created by the glaciers of the last Ice Age. Such glaciers scour out the ground below them as they move, deepening the already existing valleys enclosed by ridges. In the classic hollow – such as Cwm Glas (the blue hollow) – the glacier eats its way back towards its head, creating a steep cliff. The cwm so formed then comprises a steep amphitheatre and a pair of enclosing ridges. Perhaps the most famous cwm is that on the southern flank of Everest, the Western Cwm, named by George Leigh Mallory after his beloved Welsh peaks. Cwm Glas is a paradise for plant lovers.

c   Ahead, the ridge is knife-edged, and best negotiated on its left side away from the near-vertical drop into Cwm Uchaf.

The Pinnacles stand astride the ridge and are not easily turned, but with care they can be safely crossed to reach Bwlch Coch, which separates Crib Goch from Crib-y-ddisgl. The walk to the triangulation pillar on the summit of Crib-y-ddisgl is more leisurely, with only the occasional rock step. The summit is a broad one, the view from it now dominated by the cliffs of Clogwyn y Garnedd that form the eastern face of Yr Wyddfa, as the highest peak is more correctly called.

The descent from Crib-y-ddisgl to Bwlch Glas is straightforward and from there the path follows the railway to the summit of Yr Wyddfa.

D Snowdon/Yr Wyddfa 610 543

It is thought that the name Snowdon is a very ancient one, despite its clear English origin. One explanation is that the name was applied by seafarers on the Irish Sea who saw the outline of the frequently snowy hills (the weather at that time being a little colder than today) as a welcome landmark. Certainly Llywelyn Fawr – Llywelyn the Great – was referring to himself as Dominus Snaudoniae (Lord of Snowdon) in the first third of the 13th century.

The Welsh name for the highest peak translates as The Grave, though this name is, correctly, applied only to the final pyramid. On this peak lived a giant, Rhita Fawr, whose hobby was cutting beards from passers-by, the beards being used as a cloak to ward off winter's chills. One day Rhita tried to cut off Arthur's beard, but the incensed hero cut off the giant's head. His body fell here where, in time, earth and rock covered it. It is a good story, but, as with so many folk lore tales, it is also claimed by another site – in this case Aran Benllyn in the southern part of the National Park.

From the summit, on clear days, the Lake District, the Isle of Man and the Wicklow Mountains in Ireland can be seen.

The flanks of Snowdon are home to the rainbow beetle which is found only here and in the European Alps. The beetle, which lives only above 2,000ft (600m) and feeds exclusively on wild thyme, is believed to have been marooned by the last Ice Age. The beetle is rare and only lucky or patient visitors are likely to see it. More likely to be seen are feral goats which thrive all over the high Snowdonian peaks.

d From the summit of Yr Wyddfa follow the Watkin Path to Bwlch y Saethau.

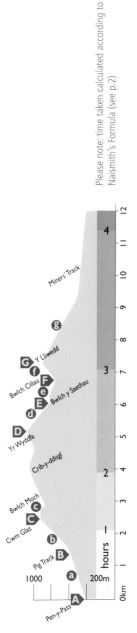

E   Bwlch y Saethau 614 543

The Pass of the Arrows, as the Welsh name translates, is where King Arthur fought his final battle when, accompanied by the last of the Knights of the Round Table, he faced Mordred, some renegade knights and an army of Saxons. Some versions of the story have the evil Mordred as Arthur's nephew, in others he is his son: it is good versus evil, the old against the young. In the battle Mordred strikes Arthur a lethal blow, but as he does Arthur splits Mordred's head with Excalibur. As is required by such stories, Mordred dies screaming, while Arthur waits quietly for his own death.

Sir Bedevere then carried the fatally wounded Arthur to the shores of Llyn Llydaw and laid him down. Ordered by the king to throw Excalibur into a named lake, Bedevere left him. Most stories have Bedevere taking the sword into Idwal or Ogwen, but they are too far away. Glaslyn is close at hand and as mysterious as the story requires. Bedevere twice hid Excalibur and was called a liar when he returned to Arthur saying he had seen nothing. On the third occasion Bedevere threw the sword and an arm rose from the lake to grasp it. The arm waved Excalibur three times and disappeared. On hearing this Arthur was content and lay quietly. Then a black boat came from out of the mist over Llyn Llydaw and the three ladies in it took the King and ferried him out into the mist. Sir

Bedevere stood up and cried out in despair. 'What will become of me now?' Arthur replied that he was going to Avalon to have his wound healed and that when Britain needed him he would come again. Then as the boat disappeared from view a low, sad cry came floating across the lake.

Sir Bedivere took the last of the knights to a cave in Lliwedd's cliff. Years later a shepherd wandering under the cliffs of Lliwedd looking for lost sheep found a cave and, when he entered it, was astonished to see a king asleep on a rock slab, a great jewelled sword beside him and knights asleep around him. Retreating, afraid, the man knocked his head on a bell and at its ring the king awoke and asked, 'Is it time?', 'No, sleep on', said the shepherd, and the king nodded. 'I will sleep on', he said, 'until it is time to rise and free my people in Britain'. The shepherd went out, and was never able to find the cave again.

e Bwlch y Saethau is wide and long and separated by a shallow outcrop from Bwlch Ciliau.

F Bwlch Ciliau 620 537
When Mordred's defeated army fled from Arthur's victorious knights they crossed Bwlch Ciliau, the Pass of Retreat.

f From Bwlch Ciliau an obvious path goes upward towards Y Lliwedd, leaving an equally obvious one (the Watkin Path) ascending from the south-west. The traverse of Y Lliwedd with its twin rock-tower summits is straightforward, although it should be borne in mind that the cliff face that falls from the summit most of the way to Llyn Llydaw is the highest in Wales. Others may be steeper, but none is as long.

Looking down on Llyn Llydaw from the summit of Y Lliwedd

G Y Lliwedd 624 533
The north-facing cliffs of Y Lliwedd, steep, though not sheer, and 1,000ft (300m) long attracted a great deal of attention in the early days of Welsh rock climbing. Here Archer Thompson, Geoffrey Winthrop Young and George Leigh Mallory (later to disappear near the summit of Everest) climbed. The guidebook to the cliff was the first such guide to have been published. Today the hard routes are elsewhere, but Lliwedd's climbs are mountain adventures and still attract a steady stream of climbers.

g Beyond the summits a conspicuous path leads gently down towards Llyn Llydaw and the Miners' Track which is followed back to the Pen-y-Pass car-park.

THE SNOWDON RANGER AND RHYD-DDU PATHS

START/FINISH:
The car park at Rhyd-Ddu (571 525). The route ascends the Rhyd-Ddu path and descends the Snowdon Ranger to arrive at the Youth Hostel (563 551) opposite which there is also a car park. Rhyd-Ddu and the Snowdon Ranger are also on a Snowdon Sherpa route

DISTANCE/ASCENT:
8 miles (13km) – but 10 miles (16km) if the connection between the Snowdon Ranger and Rhyd-Ddu is walked/ 3,300ft (1,000m)

APPROXIMATE TIME:
5½ hours

HIGHEST POINT:
3,560ft (1,085m) Snowdon (Yr Wyddfa) summit

MAPS:
Harveys Snowdonia West; OS Landranger Sheet 115; OS Outdoor Leisure Sheet 17

REFRESHMENTS:
The cafe at the summit of Snowdon. There is a full range of possibilities in Beddgelert

ADVICE:
Good paths, but sometimes rough and with loose scree in places. Route finding must be exact so be cautious in poor visibility

This route combines the two easiest routes to Snowdon's summit. But though one of the easiest to the top, the Rhyd-Ddu path is one of the least popular: often when the Miners' and Pig Tracks are crowded with walkers the Rhyd-Ddu is empty. The Snowdon Ranger also offer the advantage of a view down the cliffs of Clogwyn d'ur Arddu, one of Britain's foremost rock climbing cliffs.

Lake Ffynnon-y-gwas and the west Snowdonian peaks from the Snowdon Ranger Path

A   South Snowdon Station 571 526

The car park stands on the site of this old station of the Welsh Highland Railway which linked Porthmadog to Dinas Junction at Caernarfon, a distance of 22miles (35km) making it the longest narrow-gauge railway in Wales. The line closed in 1937. A short section was re-opened in 1980. A recent suggestion that the line be re-opened along its entire length has met with a mixed reception: it would appeal to tourists and walkers, but landowners are much less enthusiastic.

a   From the northern end of the car park, follow the track to reach a gate. Now follow an old quarry road (the round tower on the left is the old gunpowder store), ignoring a track, on the left, to Ffridd Uchaf Farm. The signed track picks a meandering way through rocks and boggy ground, passing the ruins of the Ffridd Slate Quarry on the right. Cross a stile and continue, soon reaching a gate and stile. Cross this and continue to another gate and stile and a handy painted sign on a rock. A path joins from the right here. The quarry track continues eastwards to reach the old Bwlch Cwm Llan slate quarries, but we bear left, rising steadily along an eroded path towards the edge of Cwm Clogwyn.

B   Tea Shop Ruin 592 533

In the days of guided ascents to Snowdon's summit tea was served from the hut here. It is still a good place to stop as the views – of Llyn Cwellyn and Llyn y Gadair to the east, and of Cwm Caregog to the south – are impressive.

b Continue upwards through a bleak, weatherswept landscape, the vegetation reduced to a few clumps of hardy parsley fern and clubmoss, using a kissing gate through a wall to reach the edge of Cwm Clogwyn. The most impressive part of the walk is now ahead, with the steep face of Llechog to the right and Cwm Clogwyn, to the left. Soon a junction of tracks is reached, that coming in from the right (from Yr Aran to the south) being the return route of Walk 3. Continue along Bwlch Main, the Thin Pass, a ridge as narrow as the name implies. Be cautious here if the wind is strong: the ridge is very exposed.

The ridge climbs steadily, soon reaching a junction with the Watkin Path (Walk 3 – from the right) and then ascending the final few feet to the railway station and cafe and the summit of Yr Wyddfa (see Note to Walk 1).

A train on the Snowdon Railway approaches the summit of Yr Wyddfa. The prominent rock marks the top of the Zig-zag Path

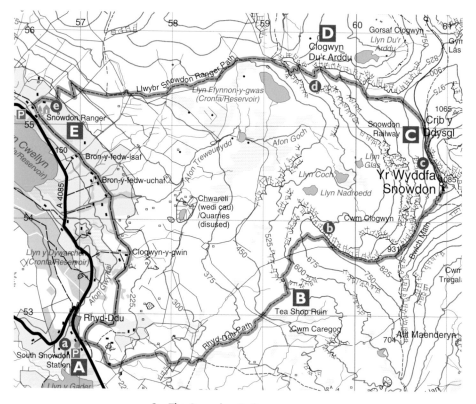

C   The Snowdon Railway

The rail link from Llanberis to the summit of Yr Wyddfa was completed in the remarkable time of thirteen months in the 1890s. The official opening on Easter Monday 1896 was marred by the only serious accident in the railway's history and one that led, sadly, to the only death to have occurred. The two trains that had travelled to the summit that day were returning when the engine of the first left the line, uncoupled itself and crashed down the mountainside. The driver and fireman were able to jump clear, landing unharmed, just before the engine crashed over the cliff edge and into Cwm Glas, narrowly missing a Scottish walker toiling up the slopes. It is said that the sight of a steam engine flying past him so unnerved the Scot that he retreated to his hotel, packed his bags and went home.

The coaches of the train detached from the engine and came to a halt, but not before one passenger, Ellis Roberts, the owner of the Padarn Lake Hotel in Llanberis, had jumped clear after seeing the fireman do likewise. Roberts was not as lucky as the crew. He broke his legs, one so badly that it caused appalling bleeding. Despite a rapid rescue he died in hospital the same evening.

The railway track is 5 miles (8km) long: the gauge 2ft 7½in (which is not amenable to metrication). The average gradient is about 1 in 7, the steepest 1 in 5½. A speed limit of 5 mph (8km/h) applies, so on a clear day the scenery can be thoroughly enjoyed.

There can be no doubt that the train's existence does allow some who would not otherwise visit the summit, the elderly and infirm, to reach it but most walkers will have mixed feelings about the whole venture, especially the cafe at the top. There have been occasions when walkers have been made to feel out of place, entering in wet weather gear and boots, to sit among the ill-clad tourists.

The cafe has a longer history than the railway, the first having been built here in about 1820 to serve tea to those who had been guided to the top. That first tea shop was of stone and, strangely, when it was replaced by larger premises these were built of wood. The wooden cafe (known as Roberts and Owens Bazaar) served food as well as tea and also offered beds. It was built in about 1890 and replaced by the train company's own cafe in 1897. That cafe, too, offered, beds. The present building dates from 1934, and offered beds until the 1939–45 War.

c   Follow the Llanberis track (northwards) to the marker post at the top of the zig-zags. From here go left down to the railway and follow this for 110 yards (100m) to a second marker post. Now take a broad path on the left – the Snowdon Ranger path – following it towards the edge of Clogwyn d'ur

Llyn Cwellyn and Mynydd Drws-y-coed from the Snowdon Ranger Path

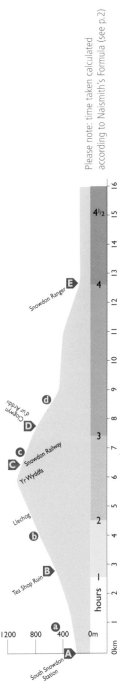

This prominent stone marks the ascent to Yr Wyddfa's summit from Bwlch Main

Arddu. To see the cliff and Llyn d'ur Arddu it is necessary to move away from the path: be cautious, the cliff is unforgiving.

D   Clogwyn d'ur Arddu 600 544

In 1798 two vicars, William Bingley, an enthusiastic amateur naturalist, and Peter Williams, the vicar of Llanberis, approached the formidable cliff of Clogwyn d'ur Arddu. Bingley was thrilled at the prospect of finding sub-Arctic flower species on the face, but it was Williams who suggested an audacious climb of what is now called the Eastern Terrace, the rising right-to-left terrace that divides the West Buttress and Boulder areas of the cliff (on the right when viewed from Llyn d'ur Arddu) from the East Buttress. Despite being severely hampered by a basket which contained their lunch as well as collected samples, and by loose rock the pair progressed up the terrace. Bingley noted that he 'had once laid hold of a piece of rock, and was in the act of raising myself upon it, when it loosened from its bed, and I should have been precipitated headlong, had I not in a moment snatched hold of a tuft of rushes, and saved myself'. Further on, Williams, with his nailed boots, forged a route up a steep section and lowered his belt for Bingley to pull on. But then the difficulties eased and the pair reached the top of the cliff without further incident.

Many have argued that this ascent of Eastern Terrace was the beginning of British rock climbing, though others see this as a little ambitious as neither of the reverend gentlemen was climbing for its own sake, but to explore the cliff's plant life. The latter point is itself arguable: Bingley notes that 'The Reverend Mr Williams ... started the wild idea of attempting to climb up the precipice ...' and it does seem that Williams was more intent on adventure than botany.

If this particular ascent were to be seen as a first it would be fitting, as the history of British rock climbing is written on the ice-sculpted walls of Clogwyn, the finest mountain cliff in Wales and one of the finest in Britain. The first real climbing route was put up by the Abraham brothers of Keswick. George Leigh Mallory, who was to achieve heroic status after his death of Everest, climbed a route in 1912; Frank Smythe and Jack Longland, who also found fame on Everest, each added a route; Colin Kirkus, the greatest climber of his era, added several more, then the brilliant, enigmatic Menlove Edwards found another. Then, in 1949, Joe Brown arrived and in a three day period climbed all the hard routes on the cliff. In 1952 he added six routes of his own, advancing the degree of difficulty on the cliff and pushing it to the forefront of British climbing. It has retained that position, for although other cliffs become the centre of attention for brief periods, Clogwyn always seems to produce something new and startling. Brown's climbing of the crux of Great Wall (though he did not complete the climb) epitomised his supremacy over the climbers of the day. Peter Crew's completion of the route showed that the younger climbers had caught up. Jerry Moffat's climb of Master's Wall in 1983 pushed standards higher. Then more recently, Johnny Dawes' ascent of Indian Face represented another major step forward in difficulty.

Non-climbers will still find Clogwyn impressive. It faces north, so spends most of its time in shadow, a massive, dark cliff brooding over the lake at its foot. Despite this northern aspect, the cliff is home to several rare species of plant. The reason is a curious layer of sedimentary rock sandwiched between the igneous rocks that produce the angular geography of the Snowdon peaks. This layer lies south-west/north-east, extending for about 7 miles (11km) and provides the lime-rich soil in which plants such as the Snowdon Lily thrive. The lily was discovered by Edward Lhuyd (1660–1709) a Welsh botanist who was among the first to interest himself in the sub-Arctic species of Snowdonia. In his honour the lily has been given the scientific name *Lloydia Serotina*. The lily clings to its Snowdonia range precariously, at the mercy of plant collector, the ill-placed foot or hand and feral goats (though usually not in that order) and its own peculiarities: it rarely grows above 2,500ft (760m), nor below 2,000ft (600m), is never seen away from the lime-rich soil (though in other parts of the world it grows happily on lime-

Walkers on Bwlch Main

The engine 'Ninian' waits at the summit of Yr Wyddfa

poor granitic soils), and is thought not to set seed in Wales, spreading only by forming new bulbs. The latter fact may, of course, explain the limited range. To many it is a non-descript plant, thin green leaves, long stems and a white flower; but to those who have sought it for years its six-petalled white flowers with their delicate pink and yellow veining, are quite beautiful. Other sub-Arctic rarities include arctic and purple saxifrage, and roseroot.

d Continue easily down the path, with great views into Cwm Clogwyn and, further away, Moel Hebog and the peaks of the Nantlle ridge. The path descends to Bwlch Cwm Brwynog, the col between Clogwyn and Moel Cynghorion, the peak to the north-west. The path now skirts Llyn Ffynnon-y-gwas – the Lake of the Fountain of (the) Youth. Is the Fountain of Youth really close by? Go past a huge boulder (Maen Bras), then through a gate. The path now levels out: continue to reach another gate beyond which the path zig-zags down steep ground. To avoid further erosion, please avoid the temptation to take short cuts.

E The Snowdon Ranger 565 550

'Fisherman!', said the elderly man contemptuously, 'not I. I am the Snowdon Ranger'. The man who suggested, wrongly, what the old man's profession was, was George Barrow whose book *Wild Wales* on his journey through the Principality in 1854 has become a classic, though his interrogator's style of questioning the folk he met is not to everyone's taste, its irritating nature, and the long dialogues, much of them invented unless he had the most extraordinary memory, unfortunately masking his genuine love of Wales and his interest in the Welsh.

Borrow was on his way from Caernarfon to Beddgelert when he met the old man and his slate-mining son-in-law. We never learn the old man's name (though he was probably John Morton, the first mountain guide on this side of Snowdon), but

The Rhyd-Ddu Path on Llechog – in the distance are the peaks of the Nantlle Ridge

The Snowdon Ranger Youth Hostel

his son-in-law tells Borrow the derivation of his title. 'A ranger means a guide ... my father-in-law is generally termed the Snowdon Ranger because he is a tip-top guide, and he has named the house after him the Snowdon Ranger'.

The old man bemoans the lack of trade, there being fewer people ascending Snowdon then he would wish as 'people in general prefer ascending Snowdon from that trumpery place Beth Gelert [sic]'. He offers to take Borrow up what is now called the Snowdon Ranger path, promises to show him a 'black lake in the frightful hollow in which the fishes have monstrous heads and little bodies, the lake on which neither swan, duck nor any kind of wildfowl was ever seen to light. Then I would show your honour the fountain of the hopping creatures, where, where ...' but Borrow cuts him off (which is sad because we might have found out what the hopping things were and where the lake is) and continues his journey to Beddgelert. Today the Snowdon Ranger, the house named by the old man, is a Youth Hostel.

e   From the Youth Hostel it may be possible to follow the trackbed of the Welsh Highland Railway back to Rhyd-Ddu, or to take the Snowdon Sherpa bus. At the time of writing the future of the railway is uncertain and it may be unavailable to walkers. If this is the case, follow a waymarked path from the Snowdon Ranger track to Rhyd-Dhu through the Glan-yr-afon (Chwareli) quarries, ensuring that you locate the footbridge over the Afon Treweunydd at the base of the quarry tip. Although it is waymarked, this route is not always easy to follow so take care.

THE WATKIN PATH AND MINERS' TRACK

START/FINISH:
The car park at Pont Bethania (628 507). If the traverse is walked the finish is at Pen-y-Pass (647 556) from where the bus can be taken back to Pont Bethania

DISTANCE/ASCENT:
8 miles (13km)/3,600ft (1,100m)

APPROXIMATE TIME:
5 hours

HIGHEST POINT:
3,560ft (1,085m) Snowdon (Yr Wyddfa) summit

MAPS:
Harveys Snowdonia West; OS Landranger Sheet 115, OS Outdoor Leisure Sheet 17

REFRESHMENTS:
The summit cafe on Snowdon and the Gorphwysfa cafe at Pen-y-Pass

ADVICE:
Good paths, but steep, rugged ascent and descent to Snowdon's summit. The ascent in particular is hard work on loose scree

The last section of the Watkin Path is the toughest way to reach Snowdon's summit, but the Path is also one of the most interesting routes to the top. The Snowdon Sherpa bus allows a full traverse of Snowdon, returning along the Miners' Track, the wide, surfaced path from Pen-y-Pass, but for those preferring a circular route an alternative return is suggested.

A   The Watkin Path
The path is named for Sir Edward Watkin, a Victorian railway magnate and Liberal MP who gave it to the nation after he had retired to a house he called 'The Chalet' in Cwm y Llan.

a   From Pont Bethania cross the main road and take the signed path for Snowdon, initially following a farm lane, but then bearing left along a rough track. The early part of the walk is through superb scenery, with the oak woods (and rhododendrons) of Parc Hafod-y-Llan on the left and the waterfalls of Afon Cwm Llan on the right. Close to the higher waterfall is a gate into the Nature Reserve.

B   The Snowdon National Nature Reserve
The Reserve covers much of the southern flank of the Snowdon range, extending to the Nantgwynant road and Llyn Gwynant to encompass the oak woodland of Parc Hafod-y-Llan and the woodlands above the lake. Parc Hafod-y-Llan is

Llyn Llydaw from the prominent stone which marks the top of the Zig-zag Path

The Zig-zag Path heading down to Glaslyn and Llyn Llydaw. Crib Goch rises above the lakes

a superb section of ancient oak wood, and the occasional lonely trees (rowan as well as oak) seen further along the route show that the wood once stretched far up Cwm y Llan. It was cleared for mining and sheep rearing, the sheep destroying attempts at regrowth in all but the most inaccessible places.

The Watkin Path traverses the Cwm y Llan section of the Nature Reserve, a valley where sheep have reduced the plant life to grasses, the most noticeable of which is mat grass, a short, tufted feather-grass which is avoided by sheep and so flourishes and spreads. On the ledges of the rock outcrops heather still grows, while the damper and steeper rock faces are home to ferns such as parsley fern and maidenhair spleenwort. The bird life of Cwm y Llan includes pied flycatchers close to the oak woodlands and ring ouzels – looking like a blackbird wearing a scarf – on the more open ground. You may also see feral goats here. The goats were originally introduced by sheep farmers, in the hope they would eat the rock ledges bare and so reduce the likelihood of sheep jumping down on the ledges from which they could not escape. The goats multiplied and are now a feature of Snowdon: they may well have reduced sheep losses, but they have certainly damaged the sub-Arctic plant life of the rock faces, the last places where many of the plants survived because of over-grazing by sheep.

A slate wall near the Gladstone Rock

b   Soon after entering the Reserve the ruins of an old copper mine are reached, on the other side of the river.

C   Copper Mines
The mill here consisted of two waterwheels and rolling ore

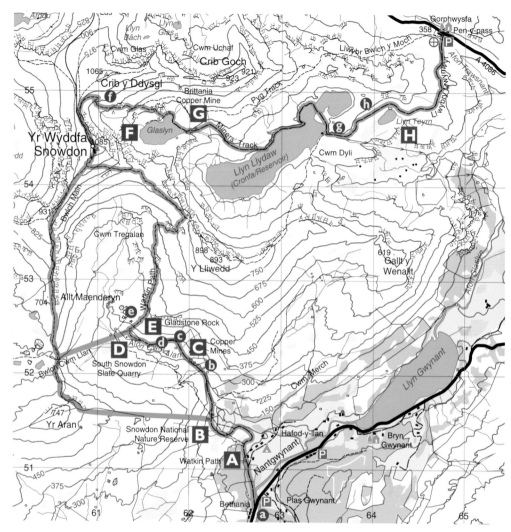

crushers, the ore being mined at three sites. Closest was Hafod-y-Llan on the hillside (Lliwedd's flank) above the mill. The others were Braich-yr-Oen, at 614 516, at the base of the eastern running ridge of Yr Aran, and Hafod-y-Porth, at 611 506, on the south-western flank of Yr Aran. All the mines began life in the mid-18th century, and lasted for little more than a century. In 1851 there was an attempt to raise £80,000 by the Hafod-y-Llan Copper and Lead Mines Company. There had been several good years – in 1847 150 tons of copper and 30 tons of lead had been exported from the mill – and the Company wanted to buy Sygun (passed on Walk

15), and to export the metal from the mines through Porthmadog. The prospectus for the Company maintained that there were good roads to the port and that 700 yards (640m) of railway had been laid down near the mill site. In reality transport was always a problem for the mines and, together with yields that were never better than ordinary, caused their closure. What remains are the ruins of the mill and other buildings including what is termed, in a drawing of 1873, a miner's barracks. There are also the curious remains of a stone-block railway heading towards Braich-yr-Oen. The railway (which has a gauge of about 4ft/1.2m) is wider than any yield the mine could ever justify and is, in any case, not continuous. What was it for?

c   Beyond the old mine workings are the remains of Plas Cwmllan, once the house of the manager of the South Snowdon Slate Quarry.

D   South Snowdon Slate Quarry 613 524

At this point the Watkin Path follows the old cart track to the South Snowdon slate quarry. The quarry began in 1840, but had closed by 1882, the cost of transporting the stone to Porthmadog being prohibitive. Stone was moved along a horse-drawn tramway to the top of the incline crossed three times by the path. From Pont Bethania, where the incline ended, the stone was again horse-hauled to the port. As with the copper mine there was talk of a railway to reduce transport costs, but the quality of the slates did not warrant the investment. Plas Cwmllan, the ruinous house to the side of the path was once the quarry manager's house, the quarrymen being housed in the barracks whose ruin can still be seen closer to the quarry itself. Plas Cwmllan is a dangerous ruin, but not all the damage has been wrought by time and the elements: the pock-marks on the walls are bullet holes dating from 1944 when the area was used for D-Day training. The house should not be explored, and caution should be exercised if you are exploring the ruin. The smooth, angular sheets of rock are beautiful, but the faces are steep and long, and the ground at the base makes a nasty landing place.

d   The gradient of the rising path eases now and a large roche moutonnée (a 'rock sheep' – the name given by French geologists to isolated boulders chamfered smooth by glacial action, and then left isolated on the hillside by the retreating glacier: from a distance the smooth rocks look like grazing sheep) is soon reached on the left. This is Gladstone Rock with its inscribed tablet.

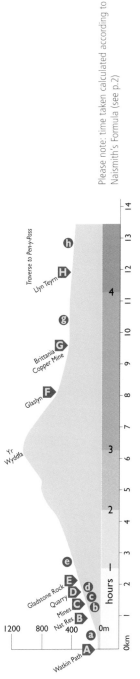

Please note: time taken calculated according to Naismith's Formula (see p.2)

E The Gladstone Rock 618 522

The Watkin path was presented to the nation for public use by Sir Edward Watkin in 1892. To open it Watkin persuaded prime minister Gladstone down from Caernarfon on 13 September. Gladstone, the Grand Old Man as he was known even then, was 84 years old and in his fourth term as Prime Minister. It was a vile day with pouring rain, but he and his wife travelled in an open car to acknowledge the cheers of the crowd. A great many people then walked, still in rain, to a rostrum where there was hymn singing and speech making. Gladstone spoke on the 'Land Question in Wales' and enjoyed the singing very much, asking for several encores. There were

Looking up Cwm Llan from near the start of the Watkin Path

cheers and the throng departed. Not one word was mentioned about the path, which since the whole thing was staged for its opening is a little sad. To make amends Sir Edward and Lady Watkin, the Gladstones and a few others followed the path the next day. Only Lady Watkin and a friend reached the summit, though many made Bwlch y Saethau. Mrs Gladstone used a donkey and there were many who wished the Grand Old Man had used it. The reason was an assault on Gladstone by a cow at Chester a little earlier. After the assault the cow was butchered and sold at a high price, the hide was stuffed and exhibited and her calf fetched good money. Many felt that if a cow which tried to kill him was worth so much then a donkey which had helped him might be worth even more.

e Ahead now are the slate tips of the old quarry, beyond which the path steepens considerably, running up to Bwlch Ciliau where Walk 1 is reached. Bear left, reversing the Horseshoe over Bwlch y Saethau and up the steep, loose and very difficult path to Snowdon's summit.

The descent route depends upon whether a return to Pont Bethania or a traverse to Pen-y-Pass is planned. For the return, go back along the ascent route for about 500ft (150m) to reach a prominent rock where a path goes off to the right. Follow this down Bwlch Main (ascended on Walk 2) to reach another path junction. Ahead is Walk 2, crossing Llechog, but we go left, following a less defined path at the head of Clogwyn Du (the cliffs to the left) to reach Bwlch Maendeyrn. The view to the left (east) from here, covering the top section of the Watkin Path to Bwlch Ciliau, is superb. Continue along the broad ridge of Allt Maendeyrn, climbing at first then descending to Bwlch Cwm Llan, with a delightful small lake on the right. A short-cut from here turns left, descending an indistinct path and, finally, an old tramway back to the Watkin Path which is then reversed to Pont Bethania.

More satisfying is to follow the wall ahead, climbing sharply to the summit of Yr Aran (a climb of about 800ft/250m). The views from Yr Aran are stunning, particularly of the Nantlle ridge – with virtually the entire ridge visible – and of Mynydd Mawr above Llyn Cwellyn. At the summit, turn left (east) and descend the ridge, bearing left with the broadening ridge to regain the Watkin Path.

For the traverse of Snowdon, descend beside the railway track to reach Bwlch Glas where the relieved faces of walkers ascending the Zig-zag Path appear on the right. Descend the path, an epic exercise in politeness as you dodge those ascending. When a path fork is reached, bear right (ignoring the Pig Track which continues ahead) to descend to Glaslyn.

F   Glaslyn 618 545

Glaslyn means the Blue Lake, a modern corruption of the old name Llyn Ffynnon Las, the Lake of the Blue Spring. Though lit by early morning sun (at which time the view across it of Clogwyn y Garnedd, Snowdon's east face, is magnificent), Glaslyn is usually a dark, sombre stretch of water, a fitting place for legends. There are many, these claiming that no animal can swim in the lake without drowning, and that anyone fishing in it will go mad. But best of all is that it is now home to the afanc, a legendary Welsh water monster. The tale is that the monster, all scales and sharp bits, lived in the Conwy river where it made a nuisance of itself by flooding the area, periodically drowning livestock and making people homeless, and readily disposing of anyone sent to kill it. The afanc was also partial to young girls one of whom, brave beyond measure, lured it from the river and cradled its hideous head in her lap. Thus relaxed it was overcome by nets and chains. The men loaded the monster on to an ox-drawn cart and hauled it towards Snowdon. Above Nantgwynant one ox strained so hard under the load that one of its eyes fell out. The socket watered copiously to cleanse itself, the tears forming Llygad yr Ych, the Ox Eye Pool. The ox team pulled on and eventually reached Glaslyn where the afanc was unloaded, and where it still lives, occasionally surfacing to frighten the wits out of a walker on the Miner's Track.

Gladstone Rock. The plaque commemorates the opening of the Watkin Path by Prime Minister Gladstone

Waterfall in Cwm Llan

With most legends it is not profitable to search for an underlying truth, but with the afanc there does seem to be a basis in truth. The beaver was once found in all major Welsh rivers, but was hunted to extinction for its pelt and meat: sadly for the animal its habit of building a dammed lodge

Bwlch Cwm Llan and Yr Aran

made it easy to find and kill. By the 10th century a beaver pelt was worth fifteen ox hides and by the 12th century it is thought to have become extinct. The Welsh name for the beaver was llostlydan (the broad-tailed one), but it was sometimes also called the efync. Were minor floods caused by breaches of beaver dam, suitably exaggerated over the centuries, the basis of the afanc story? In autumn whooper swans are often seen on the lake.

f Now follow the Miner's Track, ruggedly at first down to Llyn Llydaw, then easily along the shore of Llydaw passing the ruins of the an old copper mine and then crossing the lake by causeway.

G   Brittania Copper Mine

The mine was begun in the late 18th century (as the Snowdon mine) and worked until the 1914-18 War. At first the copper ore was man-carried from Glaslyn's shore to Bwlch Glas (between Snowdon and Crib-y-ddisgl), then put on sledges which were horse-drawn to the Snowdon Ranger (then called Saracen's Head) from where it was carried on horse-drawn carts to Caernarfon. In the early 19th century the miners' track to Pen-y-Pass was opened, which must have come as a great relief to the men employed in backpacking the ore. However, it was not until 1853 that the causeway across Llyn Llydaw was opened: until then the horse-drawn ore carts had to be loaded on to rafts for the lake crossing, a dangerous procedure. The inscribed slate slab at the causeway details the construction, noting that it was built by the Cwmdyle Rock and Green Lake Copper Mining Company, one of the earliest companies to own the mine. The Brittania Company, the most famous of the mine's owners (not least because of the eccentric spelling of the name), did not take over until 1898. The name of the causeway building company is interesting. Las or Glas means blue in Welsh, but can also mean green as the Welsh saw blue as just another shade of green, and both Glaslyn and Llyn Llydaw are tinted blue by copper leaching from the copper-rich rock of the glaciated hollows. The colour names Glaslyn, but the Welsh could have translated the name as Green Lake for the English mine owners.

g   At the far side of the causeway pause to look back to Snowdon. A Victorian mountaineer, used to climbing in Wales, was taken up the Jungfrau, in the Swiss Bernese Oberland, by his guide. At the summit he is said to have remarked that the view was almost as good as that of Snowdon across Llydaw, but spoiled by the quantity of snow.

Now continue along the motorway that is the Miner's Track, soon reaching Llyn Teyrn.

H   Llyn Teyrn 641 547

The buildings beside Llyn Teyrn are the miners' barracks for yet another copper mine, here working the copper ore of Cwm Dyli. The pipes feed water from Llyn Llydaw to the Cwm Dyli hydro-electric power station almost 1,000ft (300m) below. The station generates 5MW, fed by Snowdon's extremely high rainfall.

h   Continue along the Miners' Track to reach Pen-y-Pass.

THE GLYDER TRAVERSE

START/FINISH:
Start at the car park (720 582) reach by the road beside Joe Brown's shop in Capel Curig. This can be regained from Bethesda by use of the Snowdon Sherpa bus

DISTANCE/ASCENT:
12½ miles (20km)/4,800ft (1,460m)

APPROXIMATE TIME:
7 hours

HIGHEST POINT:
3,279ft (999m) Glyder Fawr

MAPS:
Harveys Snowdonia West (apart from descent into Bethesda); OS Landranger Sheet 115; OS Outdoor Leisure Sheet 17

REFRESHMENTS:
There are cafes in Capel Curig and Bethesda

ADVICE:
This is a long walk and adequate food and drink, as well as clothing, should be carried. The going is always reasonable, though care is needed on the descent into Bethesda. There are numerous escape possibilities into the Ogwen Valley from where the bus can be used to regain Capel Curig

Apart from the rocky pinnacle of Tryfan, and the broad mass of Elidir Fawr, which are set to the sides the Glyders are a single ridge, gently curving as it encloses one side of the Ogwen Valley and Nant Ffrancon. The traverse of the complete ridge seems to be an undertaking of epic proportions, but after the initial ascent it is, in fact, a rather gentle walk.

A   Capel Curig 721 581

There are barely enough houses in Capel Curig for it to warrant the title of hamlet, let alone village, yet its name is one of the romantic and evocative in Snowdonia, almost on a par with Llanberis as a centre for climbers and walkers. It is named for a chapel to St Curig, a Celtic saint who was the first Bishop of Dolbadarn. Curig, who lived in the 6th century, was born in Ireland, but travelled to Wales to evangelise the locals. He so impressed Maelgwyn, King of Gwynedd, that the king granted him land on which to create a llan, a holy enclave in which Curig and his followers could stay and from which they could carry out their missionary work. The llan was at Llangurig near Plynlimon, but Curig's fame as a teacher spread and it is no surprise to find that a chapel in Snowdonia was dedicated to him. The present church, dating from the 13th century, stands opposite the handful of shops which make up the village. It was 'restored' almost to oblivion by the Victorians and is now sadly neglected. It is reached by beating a path through brambles, but is locked and forlorn.

Capel Curig is the home of the National Mountain Centre, at Plas y Brenin on the road towards Beddgelert, which runs courses in climbing, skiing and canoeing. Adventure days, including these activities are also available.

a   The car park lies beyond a bridge over the Afon Llugwy whose fast, boulder-strewn waters are the haunt of dippers. The road beyond the car park is the old Ogwen Valley road: follow it to Gelli farmhouse. Beyond the farm, bear left off the track, following an indistinct path up the ridge to the first summit of the Glyders. Continue along the ridge path, heading westwards, then move north-westwards to follow the broad ridge to the summit of Gallt yr Ogof, with the cliffs of the peak's sculpted northern flank to your right,

Moel Siabod seen above Capel Curig early on the walk

Continue along the ridge path, crossing Y Foel Goch at 677 582 (2,640ft/805m) and descending gently to Llyn y Caseg-Fraith. The view of Tryfan across the lake, the peak's lower half truncated by the ridge, is delightful, and that of Bristly Ridge equally absorbing. Continue along the path, climbing the eastern ridge of Glyder Fach to join Walk 5 just below the summit. Go over, or around, the rock jumble, then do the same again with Castell y Gwynt (the Castle of the Winds) to reach Glyder Fawr. This area requires careful attention in mist.

From the peak, the high point of the Glyders, but an indistinct summit, descend, easily at first, then more steeply down a desperate scree slope to reach Llyn y Cwn (the Lake of the Dog). Walk 5 departs here, disappearing down the Devil's Kitchen, but we ascend once more following the seemingly endless path up Y Garn, a wonderful, arm-chair-shaped peak when viewed from the Ogwen Cottage.

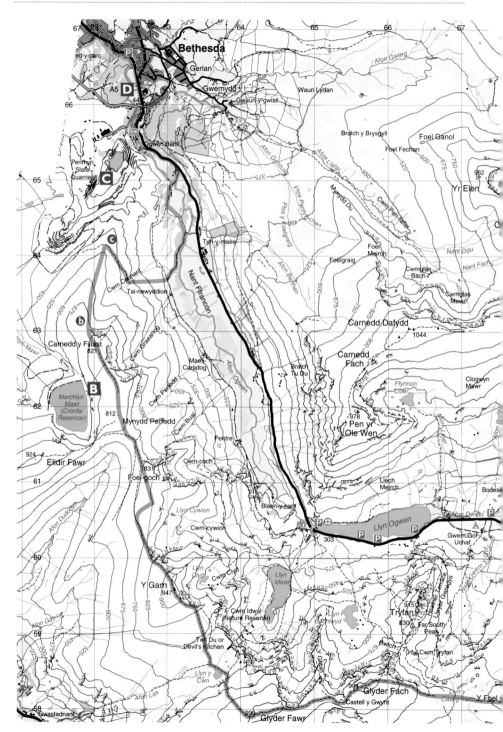

Map reproduced at 80% of acual size
1km = 2km

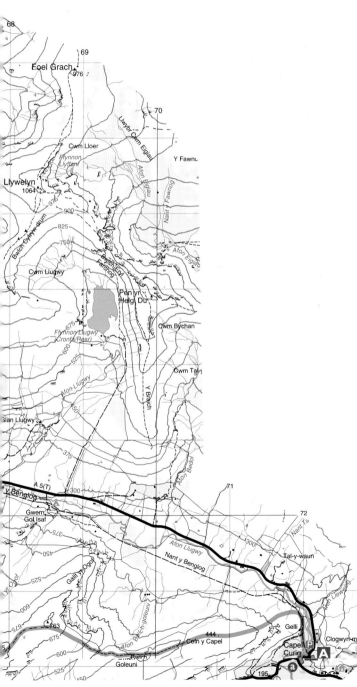

Tryfan from Llyn y Cwn

The going is easier now, with fewer, and easier, ascents and descents: continue along the ridge, heading northwards to Foel Goch. The peak's position, a little east of the main Glyder ridge line, allows a marvellous view of the ice-sculpted cwms on the range's eastern edge. Now follow the steep eastern edge of the northern Glyders to Mynydd Perfedd. From here Elidir Fawr, the westernmost peak of the Glyders (and one of the Welsh 3,000ers) lies across Marchlyn Mawr.

B   Marchlyn Mawr

Marchlyn Mawr is now a reservoir supplying water to the Dinorwig pumped-storage power station. The problem with electricity (if you are a generator of it) is that it cannot be stored and the customers are not constant, people having the inconsiderate habit of going to bed at night and switching off their televisions, cookers etc. Simplistically, to generate more power during the day you need only throw a few more shovelfuls of coal into the boiler of a coal-fired power station. But with nuclear power it is not that easy, varying the load being a slow and difficult process involving the over-riding of 'poisons' produced by the uranium fuel. Nuclear stations are therefore 'base-load', they generate constant power. Dinorwig is an attempt to overcome the dual problems of nuclear base-load and the inability to store electrical power. At night, when consumption drops, the 'excess' power from Wylfa Nuclear Power Station on Anglesey is used to pump water from Llyn Peris (at the foot of the Llanberis Pass) to Marchlyn Mawr. Then, during the day, if consumption increases the water runs back downhill, the water pumps now acting as generators. Dinorwig generates 1,320MW at full output, a power output it can achieve within ten seconds of the upper values being opened, draining 1,500 million gallons (6,000 million litres) of water from Marchlyn Mawr to the lower lake. The drain drops the water level in the top lake by 105ft (35m), leaving a tide mark around its edge. That mark is the only visible sign of the station – even at the lower level there is little to see, the power station being within the hill, in a cavern of vast dimensions. But the mark does raise the question of the acceptability of such an undertaking within the boundaries of a National Park.

Those wanting to know more about the power station – and it is an impressive feat of engineering whatever the de-merits of its construction – should visit the 'Electric Mountain' exhibition centre on the shore of Lake Padarn in Llanberis. From the centre visits can be made to the station.

b There is another fine view from the next peak, Carnedd y Filiast the last on the Glyder ridge, but from here it is northwards to the Menai Straits and Anglesey, and eastwards across Nant Ffrancon to the Carneddau. Continue along the ridge – there is still a path, but it is more indistinct now, few walkers getting this far – bearing right with it to descend towards the vast Penrhyn slate quarries.

C The Penrhyn Slate Quarries

The splitting quality of some Welsh rocks and their use in building was known from very early times. Indeed there is evidence that the Romans knew of the usefulness of slate, the fort of Segontium outside Caernarfon having been floored, and perhaps roofed, with Cambrian slate. Since the slate must have been brought at least 5 miles (8km) to the site it is inconceivable that the builders used it in preference to locally available rocks for any reason other than its usefulness. Following that usage, that is up to the second century AD, there is an absence of evidence of slate usage until we hear that Edward I stayed in a house in the Nantlle valley that was roofed in slate, and it is clear that the locals had learnt to cleave the rock. Later, when Conwy Castle was constructed the main hall

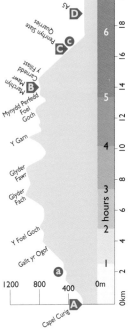

was given a slated roof by Henry le Sclatiere, his name deriving from the French *esclater* meaning 'to split'. In Welsh the rock which could be split was known as llech, but after splitting it was called sglatys, a word remarkably similar to the French, implying a common Celtic origin.

Despite the use at Conwy Castle, and other places, slate was not in general use before the 18th century, when the major quarries that characterise the Snowdonia National Park were worked in earnest. Slate beds are produced by compressive forces during earth movements. Because of the localised nature of the compressions the beds were themselves localised. There were five main areas – around Elidir Fawr at the northern end of the Glyders range where the Cambrian beds were exploited; in the Dinorwig quarries at Llanberis and the Penrhyn quarries at Bethesda; the Ordovician beds around Blaenau Ffestiniog; the Ordovician and Silurian beads around Corris to the north of Machynlleth; the Silurian beds between Corwen and Llangollen; and the Ordovician beds at Preseli in old Pembrokeshire. In addition to differences in the age of the rock comprising the slate bed there is also a considerable variation in colour, although it is sometimes necessary to see two slates of differing colour to be able to distinguish between them accurately. Colour differences also occur within a quarry, the Dinorwig rock having green, red and blue veins, each further subdivided by the colour texture or line pattern, so that there could be a silky, mottled, striped, spotted, curly or hard colour vein. Other areas were similar, though the Ffestiniog slates are almost exclusively a solid blue-grey colour.

The first development of the slate on a highly commercial basis was at the Penrhyn quarry near Bethesda. The site was owned by Richard Pennant, from the same family as the naturalist Thomas Pennant, who became the first Lord Penrhyn. The Penrhyn family built the huge and luxurious Penrhyn Castle to the east of Bangor. The luxury of the family's lifestyle, and that of the Assheton Smiths, owners of the Dinorwig quarries, at Vaynol Hall, contrasted fiercely with the conditions in which the quarrymen lived and raised their families. The difference, together with the fact that the owners were English and the quarrymen Welsh led to great bitterness. The Welsh often noted that if you stole a sheep from the mountain you were hanged, but that if you stole the mountain itself they made you a lord.

The Cantilever, one of the clitter of stones that names the Glyders

Slate quarrying was a skilled, but dangerous job involving the use of explosives and working high above the ground. The explosive used was gunpowder which produced a 'soft' explosion which did not damage the stone as much as the 'harder' bang of dynamite. In 1902 the Prince and Princess of Wales watched a special show at Dinorwig where 2 tons of powder were used to bring down 100,000 tons of rock. After it had been blasted the stone was taken to the dressing mill where it was cleaved and docked (hit with and across the grain) with giant mallets to form small blocks. These blocks were then worked by hand, no machine being capable for replicating the splitting abilities of a man. Some splitters could (and can) achieve 36 slates to the inch.

The early method of working quarries such as Penrhyn was for a group of men to 'buy' a square yardage of rock face from the owner, then to work it and 'sell' the slates back to the owner. The men had to buy gunpowder and to hire tools from the owner to work the face and if the rock was no good (for any of several reasons) the men could be out of pocket at the end of their working week. The owners refused to pay a wage on the grounds that if they did there would be no incentive for the men to work. The owners also frequently owned the only shops in the village so that the womenfolk had nowhere else to shop: to make matters worse the owners sometimes paid in tokens which could only be redeemed at their own shops. When a wage system was eventually agreed the owners declined to pay until they had sold the slate so that the men often had to work for several weeks with no wages at all. Wage disputes escalated and in July 1874 Lord Penrhyn locked his men out after a heated debate. The men, faced with no wages at all, wrote to Penrhyn pointing out their years of loyal service – one man had worked in the quarries for 60 years: the response was swift and brutal. Lord Penrhyn made three points: firstly if he gave the men more money he would not make the profit he wanted; secondly, they were an ungrateful bunch as he was already very generous; and thirdly increasing their money would bring ruin on their families (because, by implication) they would merely drink the increase. It was a typical response and one echoed in other parts of the 'establishment': when the Caernarfon MP sought compensation for men with silicosis the Penrhyn doctor claimed that far from endangering the quarrymen's health slate dust was actually beneficial.

c   As you descend the ridge you meet a cross track which finishes at Cwm Ceunant. Follow this to the old copper workings then descend directly to the lane from Ty'n-y-Maes to Llyn Ogwen. Follow the lane to where it crosses the Ogwen. On the left is a public path to Dolawen and the A5. If you wish to continue to Bethseda follow the A5; if not you can finish the walk at Ogwen Bank where there are reasonable parking facilities.

D   The A5

The main road was surveyed and built by Thomas Telford. Telford published his survey in 1817, but it was not until 1826 that the road was completed, replacing the old road which can still be followed: it runs closer to the base of the hills, on the other side of the Ogwen Falls.

Castell y Gwynt (the Castle of the Winds) from the east

TRYFAN AND BRISTLY RIDGE

START/FINISH:
The car park at 663 603, at the base of the Milestone Buttress. The Snowdon Sherpa officially stops at the Ogwen Cottage a little further down the valley, but can usually be persuaded to drop walkers off here.

DISTANCE/ASCENT:
7 miles (9.5km)/3,100ft (950m)

APPROXIMATE TIME:
6 hours

HIGHEST POINT:
3,279ft (999m) Glyder Fawr

MAPS:
Harveys Snowdonia West ; OS Landranger Sheet 115; OS Outdoor Leisure Sheet 17

REFRESHMENTS:
At the Ogwen Cottage, to the west, or Capel Curig, to the east

ADVICE:
Although route finding is straightforward the ascent of Tryfan and Bristly ridge are scrambles with exposed sections, while the descent of the Devil's Kitchen also requires a sure foot. Do not underestimate the difficulty of the walk in bad weather conditions

Tryfan is the most distinctive of all Welsh peaks, its jagged profile dominating the view along the Ogwen Valley. Its ascent, involving a little scrambling is also one of Snowdonia's most satisfying. The continuation along Bristly Ridge maintains the mountaineering feel of the route, as does the descent through the Devil's Kitchen if the full route is followed.

A   Milestone Buttress 663 603
The Buttress is named for the milestone, declaring the spot to be 10 miles from Bangor, which once stood at its base. In the history of British climbing the buttress has a famous place, being one of the earliest crags, as opposed to giant mountain cliffs, to attract climbers. The 'trade route' of the buttress, Milestone Direct, was explored as early as 1899 by OG Jones, one of the earliest heroic figures in Welsh climbing, a man who maintained that his initials meant that he was the Only Genuine Jones. During the explosion of interest in climbing during the 1960s and 70s, Milestone Buttress became passé, a cliff to be mentioned with a sneer, if mentioned at all. Then the cutting of a tree on the cliff, to produce a few feet of extreme climbing, caused a huge controversy, the 'ethical' issues it raised still being debated today. In view of the slaughter of the tree – and there were so few growing – it is interesting to note that the cliff was once so famous that it was the scene of a murder in a crime novel – *Murder on the Milestone Buttress*.

a   From the car park, cross the stile and bear left below Milestone Buttress, climbing rocky steps to round the left-hand of the steep cliffs.

B   Tryfan
Tryfan's name derives from 'three stones', a reference to the three distinct buttresses of the peak's east face. Equally obvious when viewed from the Ogwen Valley are the two upright stones on the summit of the central (and highest) buttress, Tryfan's main summit. From the valley the stones are often thought to be climbers by casual observers. The stones are known as Adam and Eve, with tradition – being, as usual, chauvinistic – maintaining Adam is the larger. Also by tradition the step from one to the other confers the Freedom

of Tryfan on the stepper. But be cautious, the east face is only a short distance away, and anyone over-balancing in that direction is likely to mean that a second step is a real lulu.

b The route is now defined by Tryfan's north ridge, which is never very wide, the best climb usually being marked by boot prints and clean streaks on the short rock faces. It is a delightful route, the scrambling never less than interesting and never dangerously exposed or difficult. At one point

Looking down Twll Du (the Devil's Kitchen)

where there is a distinct step in the ridge a step right reaches the Cannon, an inclined slab of rock which is prominent from the Ogwen Cottage side of the peak. Towards the top the ridge narrows, a final short wall being steep and requiring thought. Descend into the notch beyond and climb out to reach the central, highest, summit and the two upright monoliths of Adam and Eve.

Now descend easily along the peak's southern ridge to reach Bwlch Tryfan. Escape is easy from here – the north ridge is best avoided as a descent route as any tendency to get off route on the left brings you to the top of the Milestone Buttress. To shorten the walk either go left, descending into Cwm Tryfan and then walk north, with Tryfan's magnificent east face high above, or go right into Cwm Bochlwyd, a marvellous cwm almost filled by Llyn Bochlwyd which lies in an over-deepened hollow created by an Ice Age glacier. Follow the path which descends towards the northern tip of the lake, but before reaching the water, bear right on another path which descends towards the main road, staying well to the left of the Milestone Buttress.

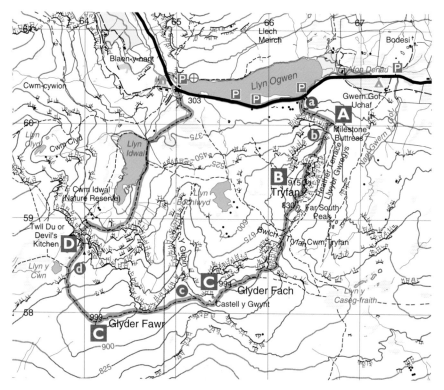

Tryfan from the A5 in the Ogwen Valley

The full route now ascends Bristly Ridge from Bwlch Tryfan. Bristly Ridge is as exposed (but not as committing) as the ascent of Crib Goch and the traverse of the Pinnacles, offering an exhilarating ascent to anyone with a head for heights. Bear right at the stone wall, following it to the base of the ridge. The route is now well-trodden: if in doubt bear left where a less exposed path threads a precarious way up loose scree. On the main ridge Great Pinnacle Gap is the only clear landmark, a sizeable notch in the ridge from where the view across Llyn Bochlwyd to Cwm Idwal and the Ogwen Valley is superb.

From the top of the ridge ascend easily to the summit of Glyder Fach, then continue over (or around) Castell y Gwynt.

C The Glyders

The word glyder is thought to derive from the Celtic word cludr meaning a rock pile, the same root giving clitter the word for a similar feature in south-west England. It is certainly an appropriate term for the jumble of rock slabs on the summit of Glyder Fach. Charles Kingsley, famous as the author of *The Water Babies* saw an 'enormous desolation, the dead bones of the eldest born of time', a bit sombre, but an interesting idea. Kingsley also noted 'a line of obelisks like giants crouching back to back', his description of the cantilever. Thomas Pennant, who climbed the peak in 1778, drew the cantilever, his drawing suggesting that it has not

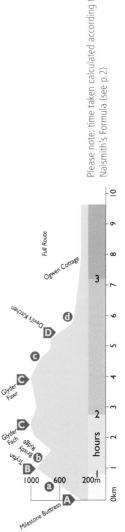

Please note: time taken calculated according to Naismith's Formula (see p.2)

Bristly Ridge in silhouette

altered in the subsequent two centuries despite the folk who have, in dozens, stood and jumped on its free end.

The next rock pile is Castell y Gwynt, the Castle of the Winds, so called because in strong winds blowing from the right direction, the hollows between the stones sing like organ pipes.

c   Soon a broad ridge is reached on the right. This is Y Gribin (The Hay Rake) which offers another short cut back to the start: descend the ridge, then, when you are level with the northern tip of Llyn Bochlwyd, bear right along a path which descends to the lake. Step over the outflow stream and descend the path from Cwm Bochlwyd, as noted above.

The main route continues over the summit of Glyder Fawr – a peak with no well-defined top, despite its status as the highest on the Glyders – then descends, at first in straightforward fashion, then more desperately, to Llyn y Cwn, the Lake of the Dog.

Looking back at Tryfan from the start of Bristly Ridge

D   The Devil's Kitchen 639 588
In Welsh the Devil's Kitchen is Twll Du, the Black Hole. It is a forbidding, though strangely beautiful place, its steep, shadowed walls wet with the water of the outflow stream from Llyn y Cwn. It seems the right place for a ghost and indeed there is one, seen by walkers at the top of the cliff on misty days. Occasionally the ghost will speak, insisting he must go on when a friendly walker, oblivious to his nature, points out the direction of the descending path. The ghost is of a man who really did go on and, in the mist, walked off the edge of the cleft, falling to his death.

d   Now be cautious. The outflow stream disappears down the Devil's Kitchen and at all costs you should avoid doing the same: about 500 ft (150m) before reaching Llyn y Cwn take the path heading north-east into a shallow, stony gully. This gully narrows and crosses the Kitchen cliffs diagonally, ending with a short scramble to the floor of Cwm Idwal (see Walk 6).

Bear right and follow the path on the eastern side of Llyn Idwal, passing below the famous Idwal slabs. Now continue over a stile and follow the broad path to the Ogwen Cottage. Turn right and follow the main road back to the start. It is easier, and more attractive, to cross the road, following the Llyn Ogwen shore line.

CWM IDWAL

This easy walk – both short and with little in the way of climbing – is also one of the very best in Snowdonia, visiting a magnificent cwm and with equally good views along the way.

Looking across Llyn Idwal to the Idwal Slabs and Y Gribin

A   Cwm Idwal

Cwm Idwal is the most accessible cwm (or corrie) in Britain, and also one of the most beautiful. Geologically it is a textbook glacial hollow, a fact that makes it surprising that when Charles Darwin and Professor Adam Sedgwick visited it in 1831 they failed to spot the obvious. Darwin later wrote 'we spent many hours in Cwm Idwal, examining all the rocks with great care, as Sedgwick was anxious to find fossils … but neither of us saw a trace of the wonderful glacial phenomena all around us; we simply did not notice the plainly scored rocks, the perched boulders, the lateral and terminal moraine'. Later, when he wrote a paper in Philosophical Magazine, Darwin noted that a house burnt down by fire could not have told its story more plainly than Cwm Idwal. But Sedgwick did not believe in the glacial theory and this may have prompted Darwin's blindness. Sedgwick died in 1873, over 40 years after the visit and was denying the theory until the end.

All the features mentioned by Darwin are still visible, the chamfered, smoothed rocks of Idwal slabs, on the eastern edge of the lake, the roches moutonnées, perched boulders deposited by retreating glaciers, their faces rubbed smooth. The name derives from the idea of a French geologist that the boulders, randomly scattered across a hillside, looked like sheep. Llyn Idwal is formed behind a dam of terminal moraine, the ground-up rock debris carried by a glacier and deposited at its toe. Llyn Idwal is the archetypal lake formed in a moraine-dammed glacial hollow. It is a shallow lake, never much deeper than about 10ft (3.5m) – though 35ft (11m) is its deepest – and in places much shallower.

The lake's (and cwm's) name is from Idwal, son of Owain Gwynedd, the 12th century Prince of Gwynedd (and grandfather of Llywelyn ap Iorwerth – Llywelyn the Great). Idwal was a brilliant scholar, but no soldier, so when Owain set off on a campaign in Powys (either against the Prince of Powys or against the Normans as it is known that Owain pushed them back from Gwynedd's borders) he left the boy in

The brooding cliffs of the Devil's Kitchen

the care of his cousin Nefydd. Nefydd, who lived near Cwm Idwal, was a vain man who called himself Nefydd Hardd, Nefydd the Beautiful, and had hoped that his own son Dunawd would inherit his looks and scholarly ambitions. Sadly Dunawd did neither, and Idwal's arrival only served to highlight the boy's poverty of intellect and appearance. Seething with jealousy Nefydd persuaded Dunawd to push Idwal into the lake one day as they walked beside it. Idwal could not swim, and drowned. Owain suspected Nefydd, but was never able to prove that he had ordered Dunawd – who readily confessed, being too stupid to lie, but, equally, too stupid to be believed when he accused his father – to kill Idwal. Owain therefore banished Nefydd and Dunawd from Gwynedd and named the lake after his beloved son.

Perhaps it was with this story in mind that Thomas Pennant wrote, in 1778, that Cwm Idwal was a 'fit place to inspire murderous thoughts, environed with horrible precipices, shading a lake lodged in its bottom'. Others have also commented on the cwm's chilled atmosphere: the locals say that no birds ever fly across the lake because of Idwal's restless spirit, and legend has it that on still, misty days a despairing groaning can be heard from the lake. But on kinder days Cwm Idwal is dramatically beautiful.

a From the Ogwen Cottage follow the well-signed, constructed path which soon crosses a footbridge over the outflow from Llyn Idwal. Continue along the clear, wide path to reach a gate into the National Nature Reserve.

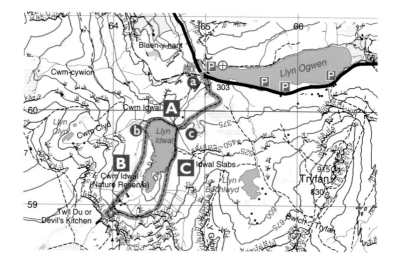

Tryfan from across Llyn Idwal

B   Cwm Idwal Nature Reserve

The Cwm Idwal National Nature Reserve was the first to be established in Wales, in 1954. One of the most interesting aspects of the Reserve is the use of enclosures to explore the effect of sheep and feral goat grazing on the area's plant life. At the northern end of the lake this work has shown that excluding the grazers allows common heather (*calluna vulgaris*) bell heather and purple moor-grass to re-colonise, while at the southern end re-colonisation is by tufted hair grass and yarrow. Close to the lake there are many bog plant species, most exotically the insectivorous common sundew, and common butterwort, but also marsh cinquefoil and bogbean. On the southern side of the cwm, on the rocks near the waterfall, on the ledges and in the crevices, of the Devil's Kitchen, the ancient sub-Arctic flora has survived the ravages of sheep and goats. Viewing specimens can be tricky and may need binoculars, but lucky visitors will spot Snowdon lily, rockrose, red campion, purple saxifrage and mountain sorrel, as well as lush patches of mosses and clumps of green spleenwort and alpine meadowrue.

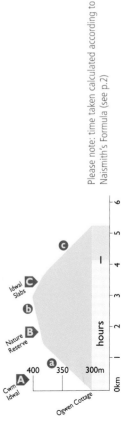

Please note: time taken calculated according to Naismith's Formula (see p.2)

Despite the legend, Llyn Idwal does see overflying birds and, in winter, resident groups of goldeneye, pochard and whooper swans. Its fish life also occasionally attracts curiosities such as herons and cormorants. Of the animal life, sheep and feral goats are likely to be all that one sees, though the path down the Devil's Kitchen (taken by Walk 5) is known as Llwybr Carw, the deer path, suggesting a richer fauna in ancient times.

The path towards the Devil's Kitchen

The classic view of Cwm Idwal, with the slabs to the left and the Devil's Kitchen in the centre, beyond the lake

b Beyond the gate follow the path that runs close to the lake to the north and east, but runs wide to the left and south: the choice of which way round you decide to go is really immaterial, but on the way be sure to notice the Idwal slabs (on the left when viewing the cwm from the stile, and the Devil's Kitchen (in Welsh Twll Du, the Black Hole) in the cwm's back wall.

C Idwal Slabs 644 589

The slabs are deceptively easy-angled, the climbs on them being harder than they look and also being both long and very polished, the rock chaffed by the boots of thousands. On the northern (left when viewed from the lake) retaining wall of the slabs the first rock climb to have been given the grading 'Extremely Severe' was climbed in 1945. It was given the name Suicide Wall, which must have encouraged those who were tempted to try it.

c To return to the start, reverse the outward route from the entrance stile of the Reserve.

CWM LLAFAR AND THE HIGH CARNEDDS

START/FINISH:
Bethesda. There is a car park at 622 667 on the southern side of the A5 (the High Street), a delightfully positioned parking place overlooking the Afon Ogwen. Bethesda is on bus routes linking Bangor and Betws-y-Coed

DISTANCE/ASCENT:
8½ miles (14km)/3,300ft (1,000m)

APPROXIMATE TIME:
5 hours

HIGHEST POINT:
3,485ft (1,044m) Carnedd Llywelyn

MAPS:
Harveys Snowdonia North; OS Landranger Sheet 115, OS Outdoor Leisure Sheet 17

REFRESHMENTS:
There is a choice of venues in Bethesda

ADVICE:
A reasonably easy walk on grass and grassy paths. The ascent to the high ridge involves some scrambling, though this can be avoided

The high Carnedd peaks dominate the northern skyline, above Llyn Ogwen, and most walkers ticking them off approach either up Pen yr Ole Wen – one of the hardest walking routes in Snowdonia, a relentless upward slog, too steep to be comfortable, not steep enough to be a real scramble – or from Pen Llithrig y Wrach/Pen yr helgi du. Either is a fine (if, in the first case, initially dispiriting) walk. Here we explore a much less well-known route, by way of a valley that is rarely visited except by climbers on their way to Llech Du.

A Bethesda

Once packed with slate workers from the Penrhyn quarries which brood above it (see Note to Walk 4), Bethesda is now a somewhat uninspiring town, run down and sad, though there is evidence of rejuvenation in the refurbishment of some of the better terraces of cottages at the northern end. The town is named for the Bethesda Chapel in the High Street, one of several imposing non-conformist chapels. At the time of the disputes between the slate workers and Lord Penrhyn the established church took the owner's side, but the chapel ministers kept faith with their flock. Today Bethesda Chapel, once sadly neglected and vandalised, is being refurbished as flats for folk over 55 years of age. Further along High Street, the Jerusalem Chapel is a massive building, more like a town hall with its fronting of parkland and the town's 1939–45 War memorial.

a   From the car park go up to the High Street and turn right. Pass Bethesda Chapel, to the right, and turn first left (this is Allt Penbryn, but the nameplate is reached later on). Walk up the street, with the vast Jerusalem Chapel to the right, bearing right with the road where a fork goes left. To the right now is Glan Ogwen Church.

B Glan Ogwen Church 625 667

The church was built in 1856 with, in part, money given by Queen Victoria to Lord Penrhyn. As a result of this bequest the Queen's crest is included at the top of the stained glass window at the southern (tower or town) end. The church is the only one in Wales with the crest (and one of only 4 in Britain – two in England and one in Scotland). The inside is pleasant with some elegant touches – the font and the neat rows of pews. Outside the 1914–18 War memorial, constructed around a natural boulder is very affecting, as are the rows of polished purple gravestones among the vegetation.

b Follow the road across a junction and then over a noisy stream – its beauty marred by thrown rubbish and a scruffy quarry, but look for the maidenhair spleenwort and rusty-back fern in the wall. Follow the road across another junction, then on past Caban Gerlan, on the left.

C Caban Gerlan 631 665

The 19th century Gerlan school is now being refurbished as a community centre. The new purple slate hung frontage is very appealing.

c Follow the road to its end and go over the stile to the right of the waterworks gate. Walk to the top left-hand corner of the field beyond and cross another stile. Now go over yet another stile to reach open country. The route is boggy at first, but soon a drier path is reached. Few come this way and the path, though reasonable, is not well-trodden. It hardly matters: the route is clear, following the southern bank of the Afon Llafar – the aptly named murmuring river – as it meanders its way down its wildly beautiful valley.

The summit of Yr Elen

The route gains height steadily, but then flattens as it approaches a tighter valley. Ahead now are the vast cliffs of Ysgolion Duon, the Black Ladders, too broken to be of exciting interest to rock climbers, but one of Wales' finest winter (ie. ice) climbing areas, the tight, north-facing amphitheatre seeing little sun in winter and harbouring the cold like the best of refrigerators. But if Ysgolion Duon is of scant interest to the rock climber, the same cannot be said of Llech Du (to the right of the Ladders) a steep, continuous cliff which has climbs of the highest quality.

There are two choices for the ascent to Carnedd Dafydd from here. The first breaks right from the valley early, climbing the obvious grassy ridge to the right of the cliffs: follow this ridge to the summit, bearing left along the head of Cwm Llafar in the final section of the climb. The alternative ascent is more adventurous, involving some scrambling as it follows the

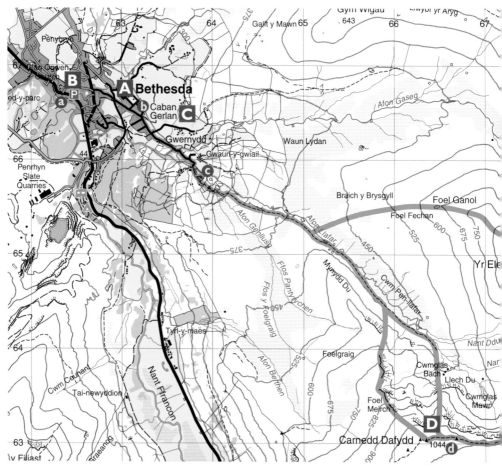

broken cliffs and gullies immediately right of Llech Du: do not attempt this route unless you are happy with a degree of exposure and picking a way up slippery, none-too-stable terrain.

D The High Carnedds

The two high Carnedd peaks are named for Llywelyn ap Gruffudd (Llywelyn the Last) and his brother Dafydd. The mountains of Snowdonia and the atrocious weather they occasionally accumulated, were a defensive barrier for the Welsh kingdom of Gwynedd as fine as any man could devise. Behind the hills was Anglesey, the kingdom's granary. Fed from the island and defended from surprise attacks by Snowdonia, Gwynedd was the greatest of the Welsh kingdoms. Yet its princes could never unify the country so that Wales could present a united front to invaders. The Celtics were a tribal folk, with loose alliances formed around strong leaders.

When these leaders died tribal wars often followed as factions formed around their sons or other heroic warriors. Those that attempted to unify the country did so by a combination of politically inspired marriage and conquest, and the brew of mistrust and violence these elements created rarely survived a leader's death or any strategic setback. The history of medieval Wales is littered with men who called themselves rulers of the entire country, but who were not: Maelgwn the Dragon, a huge man with an apparently limitless capacity for violence; Rhodri Mawr; Hywel Dda, Hywel the Good, who codified Welsh law. Gruffudd ap Llywelyn did unify the country, but then probed across Offa's Dyke and was promptly defeated by Earl Harold Godwinson, the Harold who would die at Hastings.

The Normans who defeated Harold represented a real threat to the Welsh. The Saxons had been content to police the border, letting the Welsh carry on with their tribal disputes, but the Normans wanted to push the border westwards. The common enemy could have been a unifying force for the Welsh, but it was not to be. Owain Gwynedd pushed the Normans back in the

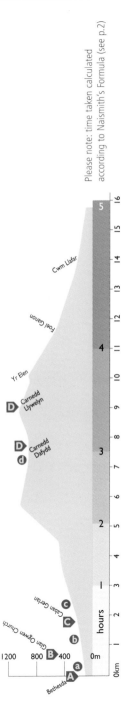

Please note: time taken calculated according to Naismith's Formula (see p.2)

The summit of Carnedd Llywelyn, the highest peak of the Carneddau

north, but neither controlled the south nor persuaded the southern princes to assist. When the Normans pushed back Owain was defeated. The rivalries of Owain's son fragmented the north, but his grandson Llywelyn ap Iorwerth (Llywelyn the Great) unified Gwynedd. He conquered Powys, sided with the barons against King John and won rights for Wales in Magna Carta. His death also caused fragmentation but his grandson, Llywelyn ap Gruffudd, made Gwynedd strong again. He demanded the title Prince of Wales from the weak English king Henry III and was granted it at the Treaty of Montgomery in 1267.

But 10 years later Edward I was on the throne, a man of much sterner stuff. He invaded Wales forcing Llywelyn to pay homage. The Treaty of Aberconwy removed Llywelyn's title, a loss over which he brooded for five long years. Finally Llywelyn took up arms again, but in a minor skirmish near Builth Wells he became separated from his men. The lost Llywelyn met a solitary English soldier and was killed in a hasty fight. Only when the soldier returned to his camp was the significance of his duel realised: the English returned to the body and cut off Llywelyn's head to exhibit on a pole in London. The Welsh whisked the body away, though its resting place is not known. In the ensuing mopping up of Welsh pockets of resistance Llywelyn's brother Dafydd was caught and ignobly hanged as a traitor to the English throne.

Edward I threw his Ring of Stone around Gwynedd, the castles of Conwy, Caernarfon and Harlech on the mainland and Beaumaris to control Anglesey. Edward also destroyed the lineage of the royal house of Gwynedd, forcing women into nunneries and killing or imprisoning the men. Llywelyn ap

Gryffudd was, and has become known as, Llywelyn the Last. The high Carnedds remember Llywelyn and Dafydd, though quite why those two peaks were chosen is not known.

d From Carnedd Dafydd follow the well-worn path around the top of Ysgolion Duon, descending to the narrow col/ridge of Bwlch Cyfryw Drum and then ascending to the summit of Carnedd Llywelyn. For being the third highest Welsh peak, Carnedd Llywelyn is, frankly, disappointing, its summit plateau-like rather than spiky, more in keeping with the generally perceived view of the Carneddau as a series of whale-back ridges.

From Carnedd Llywelyn head north-west across the summit plateau, eventually reaching a path that is followed to Yr Elen. For those completing the Welsh 3000ers, the classic challenge walk that visits the summit of all fourteen 3,000 foot peaks, Yr Elen is a time (and energy) consuming nuisance, an out-and-back ridge. But for those climbing the peak for its own sake it is a marvellous place, its position to the north of the main Carneddau ridge making it an excellent viewpoint. On this route it is a particularly attractive viewpoint as the view takes in virtually the entire route.

From Yr Elen, descend the broad ridge of Foel Ganol which heads north of due west, eventually dropping down to the Afon Llafar which in all but the wettest weather is easily crossed. If the rivers are high then there is a right of way through Gwan-y-gwiail Farm; you may be challenged but ignore it. Now reverse the outward route back to Bethesda.

Yr Elen and Cwm Llafar from near Bethesda

LLYN CRAFNANT AND LLYN GEIRIONYDD

START/FINISH:
Trefriw. There is roadside car park along the road opposite the Woollen Mill. Buses running between Llandudno and Llanrwst stop at Trefriw every 30 minutes. Nearby Llanrwst is served by trains linking Llandudno Junction with Betws-y-Coed. The walk is shortened by 2½miles (4km) if the car park at 763 604 is used

DISTANCE/ASCENT:
8 miles (13km)/1,000ft (300m)

APPROXIMATE TIME:
4 hours

HIGHEST POINT:
1,000ft (300m), in the forest between the lakes

MAPS:
Harveys Snowdonia North; OS Landranger Sheet 115, OS Outdoor Leisure Sheet 17

REFRESHMENTS:
There is a cafe at the Woollen Mill in Trefriw and at the Spa

ADVICE:
A moderate walk with some reasonable uphill sections

Many walkers are tempted by the high Carneddau peaks, the string of 3,000ers that form the main ridge, but there is fine country away from the high tops. This walk, in the south of the range, has stunning views of rugged, unspoilt country and a mix of terrain – forest, rocky paths and lakeside.

A Trefriw

A short distance north of the village are the buildings of Trefriw Spa. The mineral spring is believed to have been discovered by legionnaires of Rome's 20th legion which had its headquarters at Caerhun. During the golden era of spas the waters, which have a high iron and sulphur content, were recommended for all manner of ills. Buildings dating from around 1700 through to the late 19th century can be visited on a self-guided tour and the active minerals can be bought in sachets for those feeling listless due to a lack of iron. As the sachet's contents must be mixed with water this is as close as you will ever come to seeing dehydrated water.

Trefriw Woollen Mill incorporates an old pandy, a fulling mill where the water of a fast flowing stream was used during the cleansing process of cloth woven by cottage workers. The original pandy is a warehouse of the present mill. Visitors can watch today's weaving process and buy finished articles.

a From the car park walk up to the main village road (ie towards the mill). Turn left along the road, then right just beyond the school, following the lane around a left-hand bend. Now, before a right-hand bend, turn left along a narrow lane, following it uphill. When the lane turns sharp left, go ahead along a path to reach another lane. Turn right but, soon, fork left along a signed footpath. Follow a path through beautiful country with an expanding view of the Carneddau (take care as this does become very narrow). Beyond a gate, bear right and follow a wall to another gate. Now bear right, crossing a stream and two ladder stiles to reach a road by Llyn Geirionydd.

B Llyn Geirionydd

The waters of Llyn Geirionydd are amazingly clear, but in this case the clarity does not indicate purity. Above the lake, to the south, on the edge of what is now the Gwydr Forest there were once lead mines, run off from the mine spoil having contaminated the lake and killed off most of the plant and animal life.

b Go through a kissing gate and walk along the lake's northern tip, passing the Taliesin Monument.

C Taliesin Monument 764 615

There is no definite historical evidence of the existence of Taliesin, but an analysis of the texts that make up the Book of Taliesin and other poems and stories assigned to him suggest that if he was a real person rather than an amalgam of several

Llyn Geirionydd

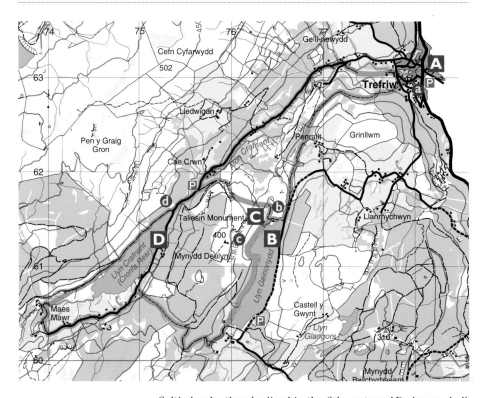

Celtic bards, then he lived in the 6th century AD. As we shall see on Walk 21 there is a legend about his birth which might imply that he is a mythical figure. Some of his work suggests an Irish influence, confirming a tradition that he was captured by pirates and taken to Ireland as a young man spending several years there before escaping and returning to Wales where he became bard to King Uryen Rheged, or to his son Elffin. Also by tradition, Taliesin lived for a time at the northern end of Llyn Geirionydd. Most exciting for certain scholars is the legend of Taliesin spending time at the court of King Arthur. While the existence of Arthur rests on very limited evidence, if he existed then he was almost certainly a 6th century warlord and would equally certainly have had a resident bard. Are Taliesin's poems on the epic adventures of Arthur – while clearly exaggerations, and a mix of magic and reality – based, in part, on the real man? Taliesin is said to be buried at the village of Taliesin midway between Machynlleth and Aberystwyth beneath a mound surrounded by a stone circle. It is this mound which is the site of the first ever legend that a man who spends a night there will be either a poet or a madman when he wakes in the morning.

Taliesin's poetry exists in 11th century manuscripts and tells of the mystical adventures of Arthur, of other Celtic myths involving boars with supernatural powers, magical cauldrons, magicians and demons, and a series of enigmatic verses which have yet to be fully unravelled but which are believed to deal with the beliefs and prophecies of the druids. There are also the epic bardic verses of King Uryen which convey the Celtic tradition of the King as heroic warrior, protector of his people. Taliesin wrote Uryen's death song, one part recalling his defeat of Ida Flamdwyn, King of Northumbria:

> There was no one to equal
> This lord of the flashing sunset
> He was the reaper of enemies
> Worthy heir of this father and grandfather
> When Owain killed Flamdwyn,
> It was no greater a task
> For him than to lie sleeping.

c Continue along the path which follows the western edge of the lake, an adventurous path involving rock hopping and tree avoidance. Near the southern tip of the lake, the path bears right, away from the lake, crossing stiles to reach a track.

Looking across Llyn Crafnant to Craig Wen

Please note: time taken calculated according to Naismith's Formula (see p.2)

From the car park beside Llyn Geirionydd this track is reached by following the road to the southern end of the lake then turning right.

Bear left with the track then, just before it turns sharp right, go right along a narrow path, following it uphill into the forest. Re-cross the track twice, then join another forest track, leaving it where it bends sharp right, to maintain direction along a rocky path. At a stile, turn left and go downhill to reach a road by a telephone box. Turn left and follow the road to its end. Ahead there is a marvellous view of the southern Carneddau. The steep cliff is Clogwyn yr Eryr (Eagle Cliff), a 'modern' crag with rock climbs of a high standard.

Go through a gate and bear right along a track to reach another gate. Go through and turn right over a footbridge. Follow the path beyond, crossing a stile to reach a track. Turn right and follow the track along the edge of Llyn Crafnant to reach a road at its northern tip: there is a monument beside the road.

D Llyn Crafnant

Llyn Crafnant is now a reservoir supplying the townships of the Conwy Valley. The monument at the lake's northern tip commemorates the gift of the lake, as reservoir, to the townships by Richard James.

d Follow the road north-eastwards. To return to the Llyn Geirionydd car park: after 450 yards (500m) turn right along a forest track. Where the track turns sharp right, follow it, but then turn left immediately along a path. Cross a stile and follow the path past old mine workings. Bear right at a path fork, then right again at the next to reach the Taliesin Memorial at Llyn Geirionydd's northern tip. Now follow the path along the lake's western shore to reach the outward route.

To return to Trefriw: follow the road for about 1½ miles (2.5km). Here the Afon Crafnant, the outflow from the lake, runs close to the road. On the left is a cottage with a newly rebuilt water wheel. Cross the bridge opposite, turn left between railings and hedge and soon right through a gate. Go left across a field and continue through woodland keeping near the river bank. When Trefriw comes into view, go through a kissing gate and continue to the road. Turn left, then right to return to the village.

Ruined quarry buildings at the northern end of Llyn Crafnant

ABER FALLS

START/FINISH:
There are car parks at 662 720 and 663 719. Abergwyngregyn village is a stop on the Crosville bus linking Bangor with Llandudno

DISTANCE/ASCENT:
4½miles (7km)/800ft (250m)

APPROXIMATE TIME:
2 hours

HIGHEST POINT:
885ft (270m) on the flank of Moel Winion

MAPS:
Harveys Snowdonia North; OS Landranger Sheet 115, OS Outdoor Leisure Sheet 17

REFRESHMENTS:
There is a limited selection in Abergwyngregyn; the Aber Hotel is open all day

ADVICE:
An easy, very enjoyable walk through beautiful woodland

This short walk is one of the most popular in northern Snowdonia, following a delightful woodland path to an impressive waterfall.

Approaching Aber Falls

A   Abergwyngregyn

The break in the northern wall of the Carneddau through which the Afon Rhaedr Fawr flows to reach the sea has been strategically important for centuries. On the hillside to the south-east of the present village an array of Bronze Age burial mounds suggest man's presence for at least 3,500 years. To the east of the village is Maes y Gaer, an Iron Age hillfort set on a promontory above the river valley. The fort may still have been occupied when the Romans came this way, building a road from Canovium, their fort in the Conwy (near Caerhun) over Bwlch y Ddeufan to another fort at Gorddinag close to Aber. The Romans followed an ancient track through the hills, one which passes close to Maen y Bardol, the Poet's Stone. This Neolithic burial chamber (at 741 718) is the finest in northern Snowdonia and well worth visiting. It is a cromlech, Welsh for 'stooping stone', a term interchangeable with dolmen (also of Welsh origin) for the burial chambers which were originally covered by earth mounds (long barrows). Here the stones have been exposed by centuries of wind and rain.

Bwlch y Ddeufaen means the pass of the two stones, though it is not clear to which stones the name refers: is it the old standing stones which pre-date the Romans by many centuries, or the Roman milestones (now removed to the British Museum). The Romans came this way to reach Anglesey, seat of the Druids, the spiritual powerhouse of the Celts. Their experience in Gaul had taught the Romans that destroying the Druids would aid the conquest of Celtic Britain. Tacitus notes that when the legionnaires crossed the Menai Straits they were met by the Druids who cursed them, calling down the wrath of the Celtic gods on the invaders. The curses were no match for the short sword.

Aber Falls

Looking towards the northern Carneddau (Llwytmor Bach) from the southern end of the walk

The final site of historical note at Abergwyngregyn is the mound to the east of the village road. This is the motte of a motte and bailey castle. This early form of medieval castle consisted of a motte, a constructed earth mound topped by a wooden tower or keep, standing within a bailey, a courtyard surrounded by a bank and ditch, the bank surmounted by a fence. Later the bailey banks were replaced by a stone wall, the mound and the tower by a stone keep to create the castle of popular imagination. Motte and bailey castles were brought to Britain by the Normans, but Abergwyngregyn's castle was built by Llywelyn the Great, who was married to Joan, an illegitimate daughter of King John. During a campaign against the Norman marcher lords, Llywelyn captured William de Braose, one of the lords, holding him at Abergwyngregyn while his ransom was organised. During his captivity Joan had an affair with de Braose, a fact that did not pass unnoticed. When the ransom was paid Llywelyn held a banquet in honour of the departing de Braose, an occasion that must have thrilled the Norman lord until he discovered that the main entertainment was to be his hanging in front of the faithless Joan.

a   From the village take the road heading south (towards the hills), soon reaching the first car park, on the right. The

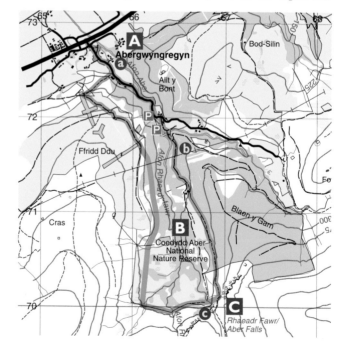

second car park is further along the road, over the bridge and to the right. Go into the first car park and go through a kissing gate signed for Aber Falls. Cross the river and a kissing gate to meet a track (coming in from the left, from the second car park). Bear right along the track, going under three sets of power lines and, soon after, reaching a house on the left. This is a Countryside Commission for Wales Interpretation Centre with excellent displays on the ecology of the valley of the Afon Rhaedr Fawr. There is also an alternative path through a plantation; this is signposted and starts 220 yards (200m) before the centre.

B   Coedydd Aber National Nature Reserve

The Reserve covers an area of natural and planted woodland around the valley of the Afon Rhaedr Fawr. In the past the woodland has been exploited by local industries, the hardwood being used for railway sleepers, the alder for clog-making, but it is now managed as a wildlife habitat. Oak, ash, hazel, birch, willow, beech, sycamore, poplar and alder still flourish, as do blackthorn and other shrub species. There are also non-native conifers – Japanese larch, Norway spruce, lodgepole pine and red cedar. Beneath the trees bluebells, primroses, wood sorrel and wood anemone flourish. The woodland is home to a wide variety of birds. In the fast flowing Afon Aber you may also see dippers.

b   Continue along the track to reach the falls.

C   Aber Falls 669 700

The falls, more correctly called Rhaedr Fawr, the big waterfall, drop 115ft (35m) over a cliff of hard rock (granophyre) which the river, cutting back its head in textbook style, has been unable to erode. It is a beautiful falls, the straight drop of water framed by the trees of the Nature Reserve.

c   Continue along the track, passing the falls on your left. Cross two stiles passing Rhaedr Fawr on the left, then just after the second, take the right-hand branch at a track fork waymarked North Wales Path. The track now climbs, offering a fine view of the valley. Go over two more stiles and pass beneath the power lines again. Beyond a third stile, take the track bearing right, steeply downhill with wonderful views to Anglesey and the Great Orme. When the track reaches an area of woodland, turn right along a waymarked path, following it to reach the road in Abergwyngregyn. If you have used a car park start, turn right and follow the road.

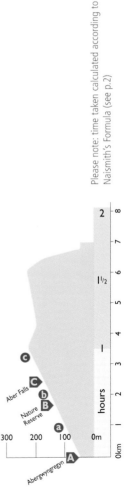

WALK 10

CWM EIGIAU

START/FINISH:
The car park at 731 663, at the end of the road from Tal-y-Bont in the Conwy Valley. There is no public transport to this point

DISTANCE/ASCENT:
7 miles (11km)/1,200ft (370m)

APPROXIMATE TIME:
4 hours

HIGHEST POINT:
2,420ft (738m) on
Cefn Tal-llyn-Eigiau

MAPS:
Harveys Snowdonia North; OS Landranger Sheet 115, OS Outdoor Leisure Sheet 17

REFRESHMENTS:
None on or near the route, but available in Dolgarrog

ADVICE:
Rugged track and a section of trackless moor

Eigiau is one of Snowdonia's wildest cwms. Rarely visited and seen only by those who leave the high Carneddau ridge (from Carnedd Llewelyn to Pen Llithrig y Wrach) to peer into it. It is therefore, as quiet as it is rugged, the walker usually sharing the magnificent scenery with the birds.

A Llyn Eigiau

Cwm Eigiau is the valley of depths or, perhaps, of oceans. The name might therefore refer to its remote position, buried in

the Carneddau, or to size of the lake (though it is no larger than several others). The lake, and Llyn Cowlyd to the south, once supplied water to a hydro-electric power station. The partially derelict dam of Llyn Eigiau collapsed in 1925, the wall of water roaring down into the valley almost destroying the village of Dolgarrog and leaving 16 folk dead.

a From the end of the road, maintain direction along the track to reach the outflow from Llyn Eigiau. Cross this and continue along the track around the far end of the dam wall. Where the track divides before reaching Hafod-y-rhiw, go right over a wooden bridge across a drainage channel. Keep along this track to cross the Afon Eigiau and continue along it to reach the quarry ruins (702 636) at the end of the track.

Cwm Eigiau from the southern end of Llyn Eigiau

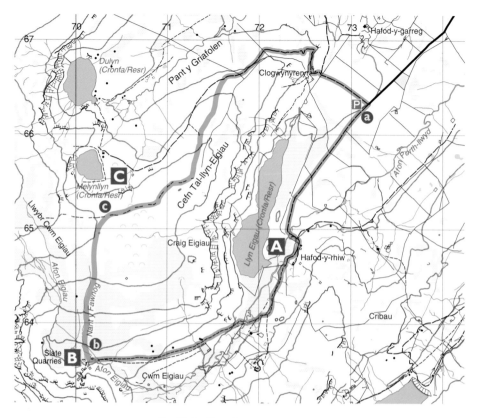

B   Slate Quarries

There are actually two quarries in the valley – Cwm Eigiau at 701 634 and Cedryn at 719 635, the latter a small site, passed early in the walk, at which there are few remains. Cedryn was connected to the shipping quay at Dolgarrog by a 3 miles (5km) tramway, an extension of which also served the Cwm Eigiau quarry, the more interesting site. The quarry was worked before 1840 and continued until early this century, with quarrying on five terraces. It is estimated that 1,000 tons of stone was shipped annually from the workings.

The site is a fine place from which to observe Cwm Eigiau's back wall. The wall comprises the Carneddau peaks which the traveller on the A5 in the Ogwen Valley sees soon after leaving Capel Curig. To the left as you look from Llyn Eigiau's southern tip is Pen Llithrig y Wrach, the Slippery Hill of the Witch. From the south the (A5 side) the hill does indeed look like a crouched figure. Bwlch Trimarchog, the Pass of the Three Horsemen separates the witch hill from Pen yr helgi-du, the Hill of the Black Hunting Dog. To the right of the summit is Craig y Isfa, an impressively steep rock face. Climbs on this crag were once the aspiration of the leading Welsh climbers: JM Archer Thomson climbed the Great Gully in 1900 and graded it XD, extremely difficult. In the usual dripping conditions it still frightens leaders who think nothing of climbing routes much further up the scale of difficulty. Then in 1952 Tony Moulam climbed Mur y Niwl, the Wall of Mists, named for the conditions on its first ascent. It is a great route and would have become a test piece, but Joe Brown was already active in the Llanberis Pass: Craig yr Isfa was becoming yesterday's crag, too remote, too broken.

b The route bears half right just as the ruins are reached, and after about 400 yards (366m) reaches a stream. Follow a faint path up the eastern side of this stream and maintain the same northerly direction up and on to a flat moorland. Continue across this moorland in the same direction until a broad grass track is reached.

C Melynllyn

Melynllyn is the highest lake in Snowdonia (though there are smaller patches of water higher) at almost 2,100 ft (640m). Its name means Yellow Lake, and beyond it is Dulyn, the black lake, a lake of mystery and legend. One story maintains that a stone pier once ran into the lake and that local folk who came on Halloween (31 October, the evening before 1 November, All Hallows' Day or All Saints' Day) would see the ghosts of those who would die during the following year walking along the pier and into the lake. The ghosts would walk past a red stone at the pier's end: if water from the lake was poured over this stone it would rain the following day. Quite why anyone should want to make it rain in one of Britain's wettest areas is a different matter. Dulyn was also thought to be the home of the Tylwyth Teg, the fair folk, the name given to fairies and other 'beautiful' elves, as opposed to ugly goblins. Lucky walkers might see one of the Tylwyth Teg, but they are more likely to see a merlin, this part of the Carneddau being one of the best areas to see these small, very fast falcons.

c Turn right along the grassy track and follow it north-eastwards along the length of the ridge Cefn Tal-llyn-Eigiau, with fine views of the two lakes and, later, towards the Conwy Valley. At the end of the ridge, keep to the left of a high stone wall and descend to a wide track below. Turn right along this track and follow it back to the start.

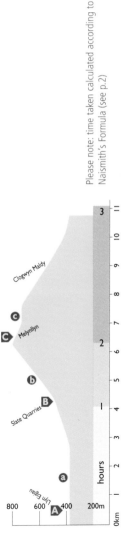

MOEL SIABOD

START/FINISH:
The lay-by car park beside the A5 at 731 571. The Snowdon Sherpa bus runs along here

DISTANCE/ASCENT:
6½ miles (10.5km)/2,450ft (750m)

APPROXIMATE TIME:
4 hours

HIGHEST POINT:
2,860ft (872m) Moel Siabod

MAPS:
Harveys Snowdonia North; OS Landranger Sheet 115, OS Outdoor Leisure Sheet 17

REFRESHMENTS:
The Ty'n y Coed Hotel, a short distance along the A5 towards Capel Curig

ADVICE:
Mainly easy-to-follow paths, but occasionally these are rough or indistinct. The ridge is rocky and can be slippery in wet weather

Travellers heading towards Capel Curig on the A5 from Betws-y-Coed round the zig-zag bend at Ty-hyll, the Ugly House, and are confronted by one of the most striking mountains in the National Park. This is Moel Siabod whose ascent from Pont Cyfyng is one of the best in Snowdonia, and whose summit offers one of the Park's finest views.

a   From the lay-by, walk back along the A5 towards Capel Curig (with a view of the Cyfyng Falls, on the left) and turn left over Pont Cyfyng. Follow the road, ignoring the first footpath on the right (passed soon after leaving the bridge), but taking the second about 110 yards (100m) from the bridge. This follows a steep farm track to Rhôs Farm where you may find a short diversion. Continue along the track to reach a fork. The left-hand branch leads to an old slate quarry, begun in the 19th century, but abandoned soon after as the slate was of poor quality and transport costs were too high.

Moel Siabod from the north-east. Snowdon can be seen in the distance

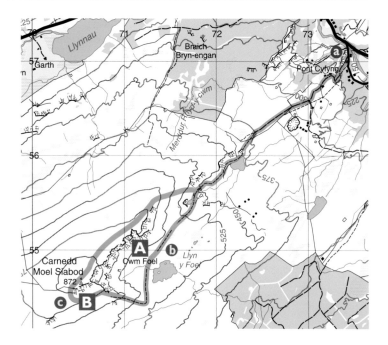

Take the right-hand branch, soon reaching a pair of ladder stiles. Cross the left-hand one and continue along a track, passing a small lake (on the left) and, further on, a water-filled quarry. Beyond, climb to a small col and an excellent view of Cwm Foel and Llyn y Foel.

A   Cwm Foel

Cwm Foel is another textbook glacial hollow. The lake, as so many in Snowdonia, is formed behind a dam of terminal moraine, and also has an island formed of moraine and boulders carried by the ice. The hollow also has a number of drumlins. These are another glacial feature, named from druim, the Gaelic word for a mound. The flow of a glacier over a thick layer of boulder clay creates a series of whale-shaped mounds producing a landscape sometimes referred to as 'basket of eggs' topography. The 'eggs' or mounds are the drumlins. On some old glacier tracks (most notably, in the British Isles, in County Down, to the south-east of Belfast) drumlin's cover vast areas. Here in Cwm Foel they are less extensive, but no less interesting.

b   Go to the right of the lake, heading for the obvious ridge of Daier Ddu, its cliffs forming the back wall of the cwm. The well-trodden path takes you easily up on to the ridge and then bears right with some minimal scrambling towards the summit of Moel Siabod, with a stupendous view on the right into Cwm Foel.

B Moel Siabod 705 546

From its summit Moel Siabod is seen to be a bit of a fake (though travellers on the A5 beyond the peak will already know this), as its beautiful, symmetrical pyramid – as seen from the east – is revealed as the front of a long ridge. Moel Siabod is similar to Cnicht, but faces east rather than west, the two being book-ends for a wild library of country. But though the peak is not as picturesque from its summit, it is a wonderful viewpoint. To the south are Dolwyddelan Castle and the Lledr Valley, but the finest view is towards Snowdon, with the horseshoe beautifully defined.

c To descend, head north-westwards along the peak's long summit ridge, then descend a clear path, with more exciting views ahead and to the right, to reach the outward route at the pair of ladder stiles. Now reverse the outward route back to the start.

Please note: time taken calculated according to Naismith's Formula (see p.2)

Moel Siabod's summit appears through the mist as a walker approaches from Pont Cyfyng

THE LLEDR VALLEY

START/FINISH:
At 736 524, roadside parking opposite the church in Dolwyddelan. The village is on the train line from Llandudno Junction to Blaenau Ffestiniog. There is also parking at the station (738 522)

DISTANCE/ASCENT:
8 miles (13km)/750ft (230m)

APPROXIMATE TIME:
4 hours

HIGHEST POINT:
1,115ft (340m) near the summit of Foel Felen

MAPS:
OS Landranger Sheet 115, OS Outdoor Leisure Sheet 16

REFRESHMENTS:
There are shops and pubs in Dolwyddelan

ADVICE:
Easy tracks and moderate climbing, but a short section of the Lledr Gorge needs care. Parts of the path can be very wet

Just a few kilometres from the Snowdonian tourist centre of Betws-y-Coed lies the Lledr Valley. It is a picturesque valley, its lower section, close to the Afon Lledr's confluence with the Afon Conwy, deeply wooded, its upper section dominated by the castle at Dolwyddelan.

A   Dolwyddelan

The village is named for St Gwyddelan, a 7th century Irish saint who built a church on Bryn y Bedd, the hillock to the west of the present building. The present church, dedicated to the saint, was built in the early 16th century by Maredudd ap Ieuan (who had re-occupied the castle), but its 7th century bell is claimed to have hung in the saint's first church. The fine carved wood rood screen also pre-dates the present building, leading historians to believe there must have been

From the bridge over the Afon Lledr Moel Siabod is seen rising above Dolwyddelan

Dolwyddelan Castle

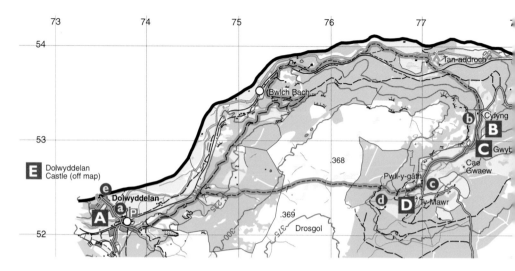

an earlier church (though later than St Gwyddelan's) on the site. The church also has a brass to Maredudd, depicting him kneeling in fully knightly armour, and a curious 'dragon' carved on a beam – look on the church's northern side. Some have suggested that the creature, which has a knotted tail and an odd, harpoon-like nose, is not a dragon, but the afanc (see Walk 3) whose activities caused flooding in the Lledr Valley as well as in that of the Afon Conwy.

Elsewhere Dolwyddelan is a pleasant, quiet village, a little spoiled by the main road which carves through it. On that road there are two excellent non-conformist chapels.

a From the village church, cross the delightful humpbacked bridge over the Afon Lledr and continue over the railway bridge. Turn left, then left again, passing a cottage and continuing uphill to reach two houses, each named for an aspect of the views they command. The view is tremendous, particularly of Moel Siabod towering above the village. Cross a stile and follow a forest track past an old slate quarry. The track is followed, through gates, for about 1½ miles (2.5km). The track turns sharply right and the farmhouse of Mur-coch is seen ahead: continue around a left-hand bend, cross over the stile or through the gate and immediately turn left through the forest to reach another track. Turn left along a rough path, passing Bwlch Bach on your right. Follow the path down to a road and follow the road over a railway bridge. Pont-y-Pant Halt (station) is up the road to the left and can be used as an alternative start.

Bear right, soon reaching Plas Hall. Here the road bears left to cross the Afon Lledr: continue ahead (to the right of Plas Hall), passing Lledr Hall and continuing along a walled track. Cross a driveway and follow the path through a gate, bearing left towards the river. Now walk between the river and the railway to reach two gates close together. The next section of the riverside path is rough and can be avoided by continuing through the plantation ahead. The right of way bears left to regain the river which is wonderfully picturesque as it races through a short gorge. The metal rungs in the gorge walls were for salmon fishermen: they are best avoided.

Follow the path as it rises from the river. At a path junction turn left to reach a stile and follow the slabbed path beyond back to the river. Go over another stile and continue to Tan-addroch Farm. At the farm the path crosses the driveway and goes through a gate passing the farm on the right. Go under a railway bridge, then cross a forest track and walk uphill, joining a track which leads to a road near Cyfyng.

B   Cyfyng 777 533

Cyfyng was once both the local chapel and the school. It is said that the children's desks were reversed on Sundays to become pews.

b   Turn right up the road, passing the lovely little falls on the Afon Wybr, on the left, and continuing to Pwll-y-gath Farm, on the right.

C   Gwybrnant

The valley of the Afon Wybr is Gwybrnant, Viper Valley. The name recalls a local story that a winged viper (more dragon than snake) lived near the falls. A local man, intent on killing the viper, asked a fortune teller in the Lledr Valley whether his quest would be successful. He was told he was doomed as he would be bitten by the viper and would break his neck in the attempt and would drown as a result of his quest. The man, assuming the fortune teller was half-witted for predicting three separate deaths stalked the viper near its lair. The viper bit him, causing him to fall from the falls. He broke his neck on the rocks at the bottom and slipped into the river where he drowned.

c   A few yards beyond Pwll-y-gath Farm the route turns right along a signed track, but many walkers will continue along the road for a further 200 yards (180m) to reach Ty Mawr.

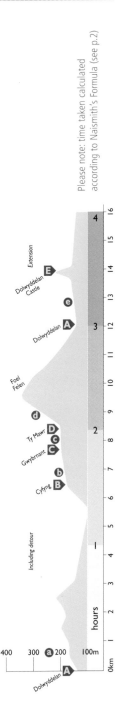

Please note: time taken calculated according to Naismith's Formula (see p.2)

D Ty Mawr 770 524

The farmhouse is the birthplace of Bishop William Morgan who translated the Bible into Welsh. He was born here sometime between 1540 and 1545 to a father who was a tenant farmer of the Gwydir Estate. The head of the Wynn family who owned Gwydir recognised the boy's intelligence and took him to the castle to be educated with his own children. Later he paid for William to go to St John's College, Cambridge to complete his education. The translation of the Bible, completed in 1588, was probably inspired by the work of William Salisbury of Llanrwst who had translated the New Testament in the early 1560s. It is acknowledged that Morgan's was the more important work, not only giving the Welsh a complete Bible for the first time, but creating a standard form of Welsh from the numerous dialects common at the time. Today Ty Mawr is owned by the National Trust and has been refurbished to look much as it did during Morgan's lifetime.

d Follow the track from the road uphill, then bear left to follow a wall (on your left) and then a walled path to reach a forest track. Turn right, then left after 10 yards (9m) and follow a path through the forest. Cross a stream and continue uphill, ignoring the main forest track to reach the top of a rise. Here, bear left, crossing another stream to reach a gated exit from the forest.

Follow the clear moorland path beyond the gate, with magnificent views of Moel Siabod and Snowdon. The path becomes indistinct, but can be followed with care: if in doubt head westwards, to reach another forest. Follow the path through this, exiting through a gate. Dolwyddelan can be seen in the valley now.

Cross a field and bear right and downhill to a waymarked path at the forest edge. Here, maintain direction going downhill to reach the track followed on the outward route. Reverse the outward route back into Dolwyddelan.

E Dolwyddelan Castle 722 523

Tradition has it that Llywelyn ap Iorwerth, Llywelyn the Great, was born at Dolwyddelan Castle, but historians doubt the veracity of this claim. They do however consider it likely that Llywelyn built the castle, placing it on a rocky outcrop above the Afon Lledr whose valley was the route from Meirionydd (the old Merionethshire, now a district of Gwynedd) to the Conwy Valley. Llywelyn's work, primarily the keep, was completed early in the 13th century and the Welsh held the castle until 18 January 1283 when Edward I's army captured it. It had been the last stronghold of followers of Llywelyn ap Gruffudd (Llywelyn the Last). Edward had little use for the castle. From his point of view it was strategically much less important than his proposed castles at Conwy, Harlech, Caernarfon and Beaumaris; the Welsh design was much less sophisticated than that of the Norman military engineers; and the castle's position, while seeming impregnable, was actually naive. Whereas Edward's new castles would be capable of supply by sea, making a siege easy to break, defenders of Dolwyddelan had little chance of re-supply. Consequently, though Edward did carry out some repair work and occupied the castle for a short time it was soon abandoned.

In 1488 Maredudd ap Ieuan re-occupied the castle, carrying out necessary repairs and adding a storey to the keep, but the castle was by then of symbolic rather than real value. Today the castle is in the hands of Cadw, the Welsh Historic Monuments organisation. It is a romantic ruin, especially when viewed against the rugged bulk of Moel Siabod.

e The walk can be extended to the castle, the main road having a pavement at first and then a reasonable verge, but car driving walkers will prefer the short drive.

Looking towards Moel Siabod and Snowdon from Foel Felen

THE NANTLLE RIDGE

START/FINISH:
Start at Rhyd-Ddu (the car park at 571 526), finish at Nebo (479 505). If you do not have two cars then the bus must be used between Nebo and Rhyd-ddu (via Caernarfon). It is best to use it for the first traverse, walking to your car. Do it the other way and any delay on your part means …

DISTANCE/ASCENT:
7½ miles (12km)/2,800ft (854m)

APPROXIMATE TIME:
5 hours

HIGHEST POINT:
2,407ft (734m) Craig Cwm Silyn

MAPS:
OS Landranger Sheet 115, OS Outdoor Leisure Sheet 17

REFRESHMENTS:
None on the route, but available in the villages of the Nantlle valley

ADVICE:
A fine ridge walk with few steep climbs and some arduous scrambling needed in places to keep to the ridge. The main difficulty is in organising the return journey

After the Snowdon Horseshoe and Tryfan/Bristly Ridge, this is the finest ridge walk in Snowdonia. Or in Wales. But it is very different from the other two, a gentle ridge with minimal scrambling. It is also linear, any attempt to make a circular route creating a very long walk whose return section destroys the character of the ridge.

a From the car park in Rhyd-Ddu, cross the A4085 with care, and go through a signed gate following the slated path beyond. Cross the left-hand of two footbridges and follow the signs by path and track to the Rhyd-Ddu–Nantlle road (B4418). Cross a stile onto the road and immediately turn left through a gate, a well-made path goes towards Y Garn – a further gate takes you into open country – now look for a rock with white arrows painted on it, take the right-hand path here and climb the ridge to Y Garn. This is the first peak of the ridge and is a superb viewpoint for Snowdon's western side and of Llyn Dywarchen.

A Llyn y Dywarchen

This is the Lake of the Floating Turf, a name it has had for at least a thousand years. Giraldus Cambrensis, Gerald of Wales, was born in Manorbier Castle, Pembrokeshire in 1146. Gerald was a cleric with both Norman and Welsh ancestry who, in 1188, accompanied Archbishop Baldwin through Wales in an effort to drum up support for the Third Crusade. Gerald's book of the trip *A Journey through Wales* and a later book *The Description of Wales* are invaluable source books on 12th century Wales, but are also rich in folklore and legend. In *A Journey* Gerald tells the story of the lake, whose name

The wonderful concave profile of Y Garn, the first peak on the Nantlle Ridge

The Nantlle Ridge from the Dyffryn Nantlle

derived from a floating island which was driven about the surface by the wind. Gerald claimed that shepherds occasionally watched in amazement as their animals, which had stepped on to the island to graze when it was touching the shore, sailed across the lake on the island, munching happily until the island 'beached' on another part of the shore and they could step off. In 1698 Edmond Halley, Astronomer Royal and discoverer of the comet which bears his name, visited the lake while touring Snowdonia to investigate the story. He is said to have swum to the island and, using a paddle, confirmed that it did indeed float and could be moved about like a boat. Unfortunately Halley left no explanation as to the creation of the island and it has now disappeared. There is an island in the centre of the lake, but that is securely anchored to the lake floor and most definitely not floating.

Llyn y Dywarchen is also famous as the site for the story of the Lady of the Lake. Or should that be one of the sites as the story is told at several places, most famously at Llyn y Fan Fach in the Brecon Beacons. The lady, one of the Tylwyth Teg (the Fair Folk – fairies) falls in love with a local shepherd and is allowed to marry him on condition that he never strikes her with iron. He does of course, accidentally with his stirrup as he lifts her on to his horse, and she returns to her own family. In the Snowdonian version of the story the lady continues to talk to the shepherd by using the floating island – which she creates – as a boat, though they can never again touch. The South Wales version of the story is more complicated involving identical sisters from whom the shepherd has to

Map reproduced at 90% of acual size
1km = 2.25cm

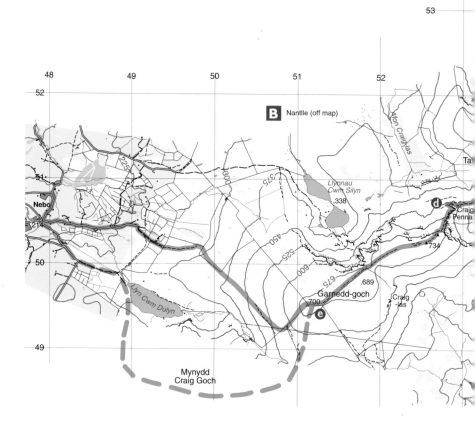

chose his bride correctly, the lady behaving inappropriately in company and being tapped by her husband (he is allowed three 'strikes' and eventually uses them up) and teaching her children herbal cures so that they become great physicians. Some historians believe the take is folklore, not myth, and recounts the meeting of the iron-using Celts with the Bronze Age Britons: the shepherd has difficulty in distinguishing the lady because all foreigners look the same; she behaves oddly because of cultural differences; she has a great understanding of herbal remedies as the older folk might have; and there is a taboo on the use of iron, the new metal. If it is indeed folklore then it is a story which is at least 3,000 years old.

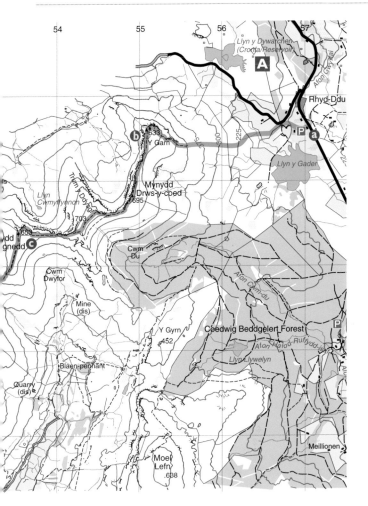

b From Y Garn, head south-west beside a wall, then continue southwards to Mynydd Drws-y-Coed. The ridge now continues in fine style, heading westwards to Trum-y-Ddysgl (keep to the path on the ridge) and on to Mynydd Tal-y-Mignedd. To the left on this section there is a marvellous view into Cwm Pennant (see Walk 17), while to the right there is an equally splendid view towards Nantlle.

B Nantlle

Although not as extensive as the workings of Llanberis, Bethesda and Blaenau Ffestiniog, Nantlle was one of the centres of the Welsh slate industry. Because the floor of the valley of the Afon Llyfni is made of slate the workings were

Looking north along the Ridge from Craig Cwm Silyn. The closest peak is Mynydd Tal-y-mignedd with Trum y Ddysgl beyond and Snowdon top right

pits, adding other difficulties to extraction of the stone – the pits were harder to excavate and flooded frequently. The stone from Nantlle was of good quality, but only the Dorothea pit, just to the west of Nantlle village, was ever consistently profitable. The Dorothea pit is now water-filled, the debris-banked water adding a strange beauty to the landscape (if you can ignore the rubbish).

Nantlle is also famous for its place in a grim story from the Mabinogion, a collection of medieval prose poems which recounts the myths and fables of the Celts of Wales. Some of the tales involve Arthur, and all involve magic and fantasy. One tells of the magician Gwydion who helps a boy Lleu (called Lleu Llawr Gyffes, Lleu Skilful Hand, because of his accurate throwing) who has been cursed and so can never marry a mortal women. Gwydion creates a bride for Lleu from the flowers of oak, broom and meadowsweet (chosen for constancy, beauty and gentleness) calling her Blodeuedd, from the Welsh for flowers. Lleu and Blodeuedd live near Trawsfynydd, and one day, during Lleu's absence, Goronwy, a local lord visits their home while he is out hunting.

Goronwy and Blodeuedd fell passionately in love and determine to kill Lleu so they can be together. But Lleu's curse means that not only can he not marry a mortal woman, but that he is difficult to kill. Goronwy throws a spear at him, but Lleu is only wounded: with a scream he turns into an eagle and flies away. Gwydion searches for the eagle, one day arriving at Nantlle where he follows a pig which has become fat mysteriously after feeding in a local wood. Gwydion sees that the pig is feeding on maggots and rotten flesh and looking into the tree sees an eagle. Every time the eagle shakes its feathers flesh and maggots fell to the ground. Gwydion sings englyns and the eagle flies down to perch on his knee. Gwydion turns the eagle back into Lleu and nurses him back to health. When he is fit he returns home to face Goronwy. Goronwy offers him land and money, but Lleu will only accept a single spear throw, just as Goronwy threw at him. Fearing for his life, Goronwy asks to be allowed to hold a stone between himself and Lleu. Lleu agrees, but so strong is his arm that his spear pierces the stone and strikes Goronwy dead. Lleu goes on to become lord of Gwynedd. Blodeuedd fled with her hand-maidens, but the maidens, frightened of being pursued by Lleu walked backwards and fell into a lake. All were drowned, the lake, near Llan Ffestiniog, now being called the Llyn Morwynion, the Lake of the Maidens. Blodeuedd survived but was turned into an owl so that her face would never again be seen by day. Her faithlessness explains why owls are mobbed by other birds.

c   Now follow the fence south-westward (crossing it twice by stile), descending to Bwlch Dros-bern, then climbing above Craig Pennant to reach a summit cairn. Note the scramble up the rocks here can be avoided by taking the path to the right of Craig Pennant which soon veers left and climbs up to reach the ridge path above the 'tricky' bit. To the right now are the cliffs of Craig Cwm Silyn with the twin lakes of Cwm Silyn below. The finest of the cliffs is Craig-yr-Ogof on which some of the great names of British climbing – Odell, Kirkus, Menlove Edwards – made first ascents. The more recent, much harder climb Crucible, is one of the great classics of Welsh rock climbing.

d   From the western end of the cliff line, bear south-west across an undulating plateau to reach Garnedd-Goch. From the summit maintain direction with a wall to your left, as the descent steepens look out for a small path on the right going north-west, take this and head for a gate and onto a green lane at 494 502 – this leads to a road – turn left and continue on to Nebo.

e   An alternative route from Garnedd-Goch, shown as a broken line on our map, can be taken to include Craig Goch, the last hill in the chain. Head south from the summit of Garnedd-Goch and then turn west onto the plateau leading to the rocky summit of Craig-Goch. From there head towards Nebo TV mast, veering gradually to the right aiming for the end of Llyn Cwm Dulyn. Cross the stile near the lakeside, follow the path past the end of the lake, through a kissing gate on to a road which takes you into Nebo village.

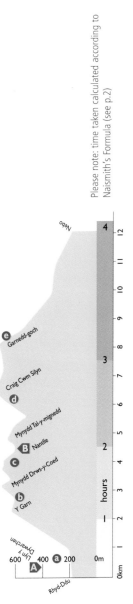

Please note: time taken calculated according to Naismith's Formula (see p.2)

CNICHT

START/FINISH:
Car parking is available at 633 485 on the road from Nantgwynant (near Pont Bethania) to Nantmor and the A4085. This road is not used by buses: the Snowdon Sherpa can be used to reach Pont Bethania, but that adds about 3¾ miles (6km) and 330ft (100m) of climbing to the route

DISTANCE/ASCENT:
5½ miles (9km)/1,650ft (500m)

APPROXIMATE TIME:
4 hours

HIGHEST POINT:
2,264ft (690m) Cnicht

MAPS:
Harveys Snowdonia West; OS Landranger Sheet 115, OS Outdoor Leisure Sheet 17

REFRESHMENTS:
None near the route: available in Beddgelert

ADVICE:
A rugged walk involving rough country and a knowledge of map and compass, but very rewarding

From the west – say from the A4085 which links Beddgelert and Penrhyndeudraeth, near the overhanging cliff of Carreg Hyll-drem – Cnicht is a shapely, conical peak well-deserving of its occasional title of the Matterhorn of Wales. The climb from the west is one of the easier ascents of a Snowdonian peak, but here we approach from the north, a more satisfying mountain walk.

a Walk along the road towards Nantmor, but soon turn left at a gate and go over a bridge along the drive to Gelli-Iago. Continue along a rough track, heading towards Cnicht.

A Cnicht 645 466

The peak's name is believed to derive from the old English word, cnight, for a knight's helmet, possibly given by sailors in Cardigan Bay who used the elegant peak as a landmark.

The view of the peak from the north is disappointing for those who know its western side. From the north it is revealed as having a long, undulating summit ridge extending back from the sharp west ridge.

To the south of the peak is Cwm Croesor. Legend has it that the valley's name is a reminder of a sad tale involving the Welsh Princess Helen who is said to have married the Roman Emperor Maximus. Helen is claimed to have persuaded her husband to build the road that bears her name – Sarn Helen – to help her people travel their country more easily. One day Helen was returning to Caernarfon with a protecting squadron of legionnaires when she stopped in this remote valley to rest and drink from a cool spring (which is still known as Ffynnon Helen, Helen's spring). Her youngest (and favourite) son, anxious to reach Caernarfon did not stop, pressing on northwards with a few soldiers. Near Llyn Cwellyn, the lake at the base of Snowdon's western flank, the giant Cidwm (for whom the crag Castell Cidwm, to the north-west of the lake, is named) attacked the party and Helen's son was killed. One of the survivors rushed back to tell Helen, reaching her while she was still resting in the valley. On being told the news Helen broke down in despair and wept 'Oh croes awr' (oh Cursed Hour), and the valley has been Croesor since that day.

b Continue along the track as it bears right (south) through wild country to reach a small lake. Now leave the track, heading south-east, towards the summit, across pathless ground: if you stray to the right, no matter – you will reach the eroded path on the peak's western ridge and can turn left to follow it to the top.

The classic view of Cnicht from the west

After enjoying the view, which is marvellous, taking in Snowdon and the Glyders, to the north, Moel Hebog to the west, Moel Siabod, to the north-east, and the Moelwyns, almost within touching distance, walk along the summit ridge

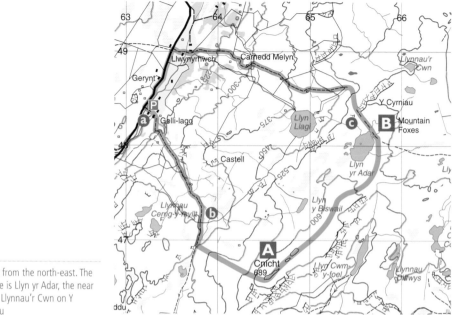

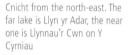

Cnicht from the north-east. The far lake is Llyn yr Adar, the near one is Llynnau'r Cwn on Y Cyrniau

Snowdon from above Y Cyrniau

and follow a path which descends towards Llyn yr Adar, with Llyn y Biswail to the left. At Llyn yr Adar the path disappears: head for the far (northern) shore of the lake, walking with it on your left, to reach a more distinct path which heads north-west. Follow this path as it turns left (west) to reach gentler sloping ground to the north of Llyn Lagi. The view from here, of the lake and the stream that feeds it from Llyn yr Adar above is worth the walk on its own.

B Mountain Foxes
Welsh hill farmers have long claimed that there are two species (sub-species in zoological terms) of fox, the 'ordinary' red fox and a larger, greyer animal which lives higher in the hills. The farmers even have different names for the types, adding to the Welsh for fox, cadno (or, sometimes, llwynog) either corgi (mongrel) for the smaller, red animal and milgi (greyhound) for the larger, grey fox. It is likely that they are really just colour variations of the one animal – but all the foxes around Cnicht (and they are not an uncommon sight) do seem to be grey and quite big.

c Continue along the well-defined path which meanders through marshy ground, then heather to reach Llwynyrhwch. Pass the house on your left and climb gently to a kissing gate. Go through and continue to reach the road. Turn left to return to the start.

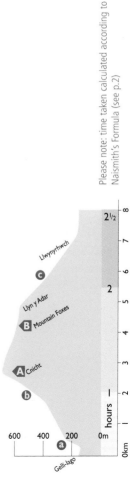

Please note: time taken calculated according to Naismith's Formula (see p.2)

ABERGLASLYN AND CWM BYCHAN

START/FINISH:
Beddgelert. The village is on several bus routes and has several car parks

DISTANCE/ASCENT:
6 miles (9.5km)/900ft (275m)

APPROXIMATE TIME:
3 hours

HIGHEST POINT:
920ft (280m) Bwlch y Sygyn

REFRESHMENTS:
All tastes are catered for in Beddgelert

MAPS:
Harveys Snowdonia West; OS Landranger Sheet 115, OS Outdoor Leisure Sheet 17

ADVICE:
An easy and entertaining walk. Take care with children as the river in Aberglaslyn is fast and close

No book on Snowdonia is complete without mention of the Aberglaslyn Pass, the magnificent gorge to the south of Beddgelert. This fine walk, arguably the best lowland walk in the National Park, traverses the pass, then follows an intriguing valley to view the most potent site in Celtic mythology.

A Beddgelert

Beddgelert (see Walk 16 for the true derivation of the name) is almost entirely a tourist village, every building seemingly given over to the sale of ice cream or souvenirs. Yet despite the commercialism it is a pretty place – the huddle of houses, the old bridge over the river. The Royal Goat Hotel is the largest building, a pleasant place once owned by David Pritchard creator of the Gelert legend. It is said that after his death in 1821 (from a heart attack at the age of 52) Pritchard's ghost was often seen wandering the village and heard moving about the hotel. Eventually an old servant plucked up the courage to wait for the ghost and to ask it why it was restless. Pritchard's ghost told the servant that his sudden death meant he had been unable to reveal the whereabouts of his hoard of gold coins to his wife, and that she would never find them without help. The ghost told the servant where to find the hoard and to tell his wife that he (the servant) was to receive a reward. It even specified the amount. The next day the hoard was duly found just where the ghost said it would be and the delighted wife duly rewarded the servant. The ghost was never seen again.

Beddgelert from Mynydd Sygyn to the south-east

Beddgelert

a From the bridge which takes the main road over the Afon Glaslyn head east to another bridge, turning just before it to follow the well trodden path beside the river. Soon, a short (equally well-trodden) detour from the path reaches Gelert's Grave.

B Gelert's Grave 590 477

In 1801 David Pritchard, the landlord of the Goat (now Royal Goat) Hotel, decided that something needed to be done to improve Beddgelert's tourist trade. He therefore invented the tale of Gelert the faithful dog – or, rather, he borrowed it as it is a tale told at many places throughout the world. Here the tale relates to Llywelyn the Great who leaves Gelert, his favourite dog, in charge of his baby son while he goes hunting. On his return, Llywelyn finds Gelert covered in blood, the baby's crib overturned and the baby nowhere to be seen. Thinking the dog has killed the baby, Llywelyn slaughters it with his sword, but then hears the baby whimpering from beneath a pile of blood-soaked bedding. Lifting the clothes he finds his son, unharmed, and the body of a wolf, killed by Gelert to protect the child. Filled with remorse Llywelyn buries Gelert and names the place for his grave – Beddgelert.

One visitor to the grave, a poet, was clearly unimpressed and left his feelings in the form of a couplet:

> Pass on O tender-hearted, dry your eyes
> Not here a greyhound, but a landlord lies.

b Continue along the path beside the river, going through several gates. The old footbridge that once spanned the river has been dismantled, but a new one will be built by the Festiniog Railway Company when the track re-opens. That will then be used to reach the footpath on the opposite bank of the river. For the time being walkers must either continue towards the A498, turning left to follow a path before the kissing gate – this path exits onto the road eventually. Continue on the pavement or road edge, taking great care, through the Aberglaslyn Pass, with stunning scenery in all directions, or return to Beddgelert, crossing the bridge there and following the Fisherman's Path on the eastern bank through the Pass. This path is occasionally rugged and is difficult at one point: the roadside path/ road is easier if care is taken.

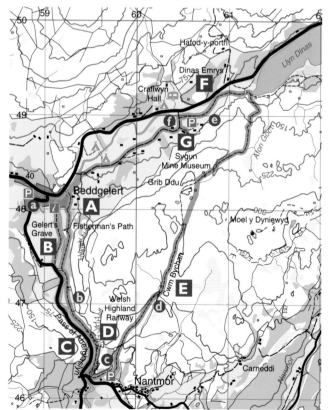

Gelert's Grave

C Aberglaslyn Pass

The name Aberglaslyn means the confluence of the Blue Lake. Usually aber refers to the point where a river meets the sea (eg. Aberystwyth) but it need not always be so: it can also mean the point where rivers meet (eg Abergavenny where the River Gavenny meets the River Usk). Here the name really does mean where the river (the Glaslyn) meets the sea, the sea once extending inland to this point. Then, in the 19th century, William Madocks built the 'cob', a causeway/sea barrier to the south, reclaiming the land behind it and so pushing the sea back almost 5 miles (8km) from Nantmor. Madocks then built a new port at the end of his cob, calling it after himself. In time the port became Portmadoc, a legend growing up that it was named for Madoc, the Welshman said to have discovered America in Celtic times. Now the name of the port has been 'Welshised' to Porthmadog.

The Pass, or gorge, of the river is one of the most photographed places in the Snowdonian National Park. And rightly so, as it is achingly beautiful, a breathtaking combination of trees and clear water racing over boulders with a background of rugged hillside.

D The Welsh Highland Railway

The Welsh Highland Railway linked Caernarfon to Porthmadog, a distance of 22 miles (35km). At first it linked Caernarfon to the Snowdon Ranger, allowing travellers to

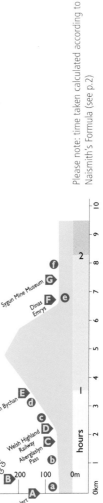

The Aberglaslyn Pass from Pont Glaslyn

reach the base of the guided trail to Snowdon's summit. This section was opened in 1881 and was highly successful until 1896 when the railway to Snowdon's summit opened. The owners then decided to push their railway through to Porthmadog to increase trade, a move which was less successful than they had hoped. The line closed in 1937 but recently permission has been given to reopen it (see b above).

c   Walkers on the east bank of the Glaslyn turn left, up steps, just before a kissing gate onto the road, following a path through a gate to reach another gate. Beyond, follow the signed path through Cwm Bychan with its array of rusting mining machinery. Walkers on the road, turn left on the

A4085, crossing the Glaslyn and turning left through the kissing gate again to regain the route.

E   Cwm Bychan

Copper mining was first recorded in Cwm Bychan in 1720 though the period of greatest working was from 1780. It was a short-lived success however: the mine had closed by about 1820. The aerial ropeway whose towers now stand like modern sculptures along the valley date from 1870 when the Cwm Buchan [sic] Silver Lead Mining Co was formed. Ore was transported on the ropeway to a crushing mill near Nantmor. The name of the company seems to have been more in hope than in fact, almost no ore being transported and little silver extracted. The company maintained at one point that they had found gold, but the venture was a failure, the mine closing in 1875. Now only the rusting towers, and a collection of equally rusty buckets and other bits among the bracken remain.

d   Ignore all turnings to reach the col ahead. The path down towards Llyn Dinas is straightforward and never particularly steep, finding a devious, terrace-like way down the hill. When you reach the western tip of Llyn Dinas, turn left along a clear path. To the right, the tree-shrouded mound is Dinas Emrys.

F   Dinas Emrys 606 491

Traditionally Dinas Emrys was the fortress of Vortigern, the king who brought Saxons to Britain to fight as mercenaries only to discover that their enthusiasm for the country meant that instead of returning home they brought their friends and relatives from Europe and drove the Britons from their own land.

A waterfall in Cwm Bychan

The towers of the old aerial ropeway still stand in Cwm Bychan

When the Saxons were driving westward across Britain legend has it that Vortigern first retreated to Dinas Emrys (before continuing westwards – see Walk 28) and set his builders to work on a tower. Each morning the builders found that their work of the previous day had disappeared. In despair Vortigern consulted his magicians who maintained that unless the earth on which the tower was to stand was soaked in the blood of a boy with no father it could never be built. In South Wales a boy whose mother had been made pregnant by an invisible half-man/half-angel was found and brought to the site, but before he could be sacrificed he told Vortigern that his magicians were liars and that the building stone was disappearing into a pool below the hill where two dragons lay sleeping. The builders dug and did indeed unearth a pool. The two dragons, one red, one white woke and began to fight, first the white winning, but then the red. Just as the red was on the point of victory it started to tear itself apart, allowing the white one to recover. The boy was Merlin, and his prophecy came true, the white (Saxon) dragon winning until Arthur appeared to halt the Saxon advance. Then the red dragon, the Britons, were victorious, but civil war between Arthur and Mordred weakened them and allowed the Saxons to advance again. Later, the story was to prove true again: united the Welsh defeated the Normans, but then wars between the kingdoms of Wales weakened them and allowed the Normans to conquer them.

Interestingly, Dinas Emrys does indeed have the ruins of a tower (probably built by Llywelyn the Great) and also evidence of an underground pool used as a reservoir by its defenders.

e   Follow the path to reach a gate into the 'compound' of the Sygun Copper Mine Museum.

G   Sygun Mine Museum
The Sygun mine was possibly opened in the late 18th century, though there is no written evidence before 1825. As with most of the other local mines it suffered from low yield and transport problems, and though it was occasionally profitable it passed through a succession of owners whose ambition exceeded their common sense. Ultimately, around 1900, the mine closed. It briefly achieved fame of an unexpected sort when the site was used as a Chinese town in the filming of *Inn of the Sixth Happiness* with Ingrid Bergman. It was then re-opened as a museum to copper mining in Snowdonia.

f   Cross the entrance road to reach another gate and follow the lane beyond towards Beddgelert. Where the lane bends right to reach the main road (the A498), continue ahead through a gate/stile crossing two stiles on the way back to the village. The outward route is joined by crossing the bridge seen early in the walk: reverse the outward route for a short distance to return to the start.

MOEL HEBOG

START/FINISH:
Beddgelert. The village is on several bus routes and has several car parks

DISTANCE/ASCENT:
6½ miles (10.5km)/2,800ft (850m)

APPROXIMATE TIME:
4 hours

HIGHEST POINT:
2,565ft (782m) Moel Hebog

MAPS:
Harveys Snowdonia West; OS Landranger Sheet 115, OS Outdoor Leisure Sheet 17. Please note OS Leisure Sheet 17 does not show the correct route up Moel Hebog; use the route shown on p.112

REFRESHMENTS:
All tastes are catered for in Beddgelert

ADVICE:
A rugged walk with paths occasionally unclear. The descent involves tricky route-finding. Only those able to scramble should visit Owain Glyndwr's Cave

Standing high above Beddgelert and remote from other peaks, Moel Hebog is an obvious target for walkers. Its position makes it a fine viewpoint, and to the north is a cave associated with Owain Glyndwr, leader of the last Welsh rebellion against the English.

Moel Hebog from Bwlch Meillionen, the col between Hebog and Moel yr Ogof

A Beddgelert

Despite the legend of Gelert and the grave at the end of the well-trodden path (see Note to Walk 15) Beddgelert almost certainly derives its name from Celert, a 5th or 6th century Celtic saint. Celert had a hermitage cell here and there was probably an early church, the village being such a holy spot that an Augustinian Priory was founded. Of the Priory, built on the western side of the Afon Glaslyn, little now remains.

a From Beddgelert, follow the A4085, with great care, towards Caernarfon for about 550 yards (500m) to reach a lane (on the left, at 585 483) for Cwm Cloch Farm. Turn right over a ladder stile and cross wet ground to reach the base of Hebog's north-eastern ridge. A rough path now follows the ridge: there is some easy scrambling towards the top and a final miserable scree slope to the summit.

Ogof Owain Glyndwr, the cave on Moel yr Ogof

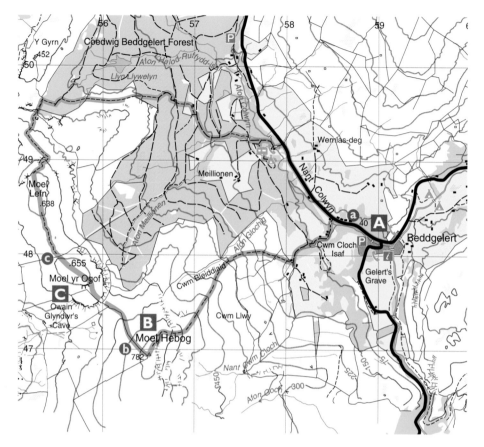

B   Moel Hebog 565 469

Moel Hebog is the Hill of the Falcon, and is one of a number of places in Snowdonia where the peregrine falcon might still be seen.

There is a marvellous panorama from the top – west into Cwm Pennant and towards the Rivals and Llyn Peninsula; the Nantlle Ridge and Snowdon to the north; east to the Moelwynion peaks and south towards Porthmadog and the coast, and the Rhinogs.

b After enjoying the view from the summit head north-westwards, descending steep grass (with a wall on your left) to reach the col between Hebog and Moel yr Ogof. Now climb the easiest route through the rock outcrops, staying right of the largest crag, to reach Moel yr Ogof's summit. Ogof Owain Glyndwr is the largest of the caves (more like rock clefts than true caves) on the peak's eastern side. A visit to the cave involves a steep scramble.

C Owain Glyndwr's Cave 559 478

Owain Glyndwr was born sometime between 1349 and 1359 and inherited estates at Sycharth and Glyndyfrdwy in Powys. In 1399, when he was at least 40 and perhaps 50, he become involved in a dispute with the Marcher lord Reginald Grey, Lord of Ruthin over a piece of land. Grey was a Norman and the court took his side, dismissing Glyndwr's claim with a contemptuous 'What care we for barefoot Welsh dogs'. Glyndwr could trace his lineage from the royal house of Powys and the insult was almost more than he could bear. Then, in 1400, Lord Grey failed to pass a message to Glyndwr from Henry IV. Henry was raising an army to campaign in Scotland and Grey, as senior Marcher lord, was required to inform his neighbours of the call. Henry's army was defeated and he turned his wrath on the Welshman, giving Grey permission to move against him. Glyndwr agreed to meet Grey, but the Norman had planned an ambush. Glyndwr's bard, Iolo Goch, warned his master in a cryptic verse, spoken in Welsh, and he escaped. Soon Glyndwr had raised a band of disgruntled Welshman: his rebellion had begun.

At first Glyndwr attacked Marcher towns – Ruthin, Flint, Hawarden – but in 1401 the Tudors of Anglesey (the family who would later supply England with a king) took Conwy Castle and in a lonely valley on Plynlimon Glyndwr's small band defeated a larger English army. By 1402 Glyndwr controlled most of north and mid-Wales and won a resounding victory at Pilleth. Welsh archers annihilating the English knights. Glyndwr then signed a pact with Henry Percy – Hotspur – to divide England and Wales after they had defeated the king. But Hotspur's army was beaten at Shrewsbury, Glyndwr's men not making to the field in time. The defeat was at the hands of an army led by Prince Henry, the king's 16 year old son. Young Henry would become Henry V, the scourge of the French. He was a fine soldier despite his youth and his campaign against Glyndwr turned the tide of the rebellion, though initially the Welshman continued to strengthen his grip on Snowdonia where he took, and lived in, Harlech Castle.

In 1404 Glyndwr felt secure enough to hold a parliament in Machynlleth, but in 1405 a string of defeats at Prince Henry's hands reduced the size of the Welsh 'kingdom'. Then, in 1406 Prince Henry retook several castles close to Snowdonia: the rebellion was over.

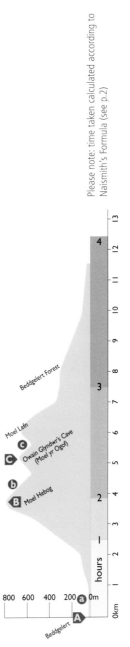

Of Owain Glyndwr nothing certain is known after 1406, nothing at all after 1412. In 1413 Prince Henry became Henry V and offered him a pardon, but there was no response. Perhaps he was already dead. The Welsh bards did not agree. Their verses maintained that, like Arthur, Glyndwr had taken the last of his men and retired to a cave in Snowdonia to await the call to rise and free Wales. The cave on this lonely hillside would be ideal for a slumbering warrior – remote, yet within sight of Snowdon's high peaks. But the name is not entirely mythical, tradition having it that in the early days of the rebellion, before he had captured Harlech castle, Glyndwr really did use caves such as this as temporary bases.

c   From Moel yr Ogof, continue north-westwards over easier ground, descending, then climbing to the summit of Moel Lefn from where there is a marvellous view of the upper section of Cwm Pennant and of the Nantlle Ridge. From here it is possible to continue along the peak line which heads north, then around the head of Cwm Pennant to reach Mynydd Tal-y-Mignedd. This fine route crosses Bwlch-y-ddwy-elor, the Pass of the Two Biers. In the days before there was a church in Cwm Pennant corpses would be carried over this pass to Rhyd-Ddu, the name commemorating the meeting, at the pass, of the bier from Pennant and that from Rhyd-ddu, villagers from the latter completing the job of carrying the corpse for burial.

From Moel Lefn head north along the ridged summit, then descend awkwardly to Bwlch Cwm-trwsgl, bearing right at first, then back left to avoid the outcrops. Turn right through a wall gap to reach a stile into Beddgelert Forest. The way is now eastwards, but the route is not clear: descend to a track,

Moel Hebog from Glyndwr's Cave

turn left along it for about 330ft (100m) to reach a cairn. Now turn right along a path, crossing a footbridge to reach a stile out of the forest. Maintain direction to reach another stile back into the forest following the blue painted posts. Continue ahead to reach a forest track and turn left along it. Follow it as it bends right, but when it bends left, continue ahead, descending to reach another forest track.

Turn right, but almost immediately left along a path. This path crosses two more forest tracks to reach a stream (569 495). Turn right onto a forest track. Continue south then east along the forest track to a T-junction (575 492), turn right to reach the camp site. Turn left and walk down to the main road (the A4085). Turn right and follow the road, with care, back to Beddgelert.

Moel Hebog and Moel yr Ogof above the Beddgelert Forest

CWM PENNANT

START/FINISH:
At 532 476 where verge parking is available on the Cwm Pennant road, just before a gated bridge. There is no public transport to Cwm Pennant

DISTANCE/ASCENT:
3½ miles (5.5km) – 425ft (130m)

APPROXIMATE TIME:
2 hours

HIGHEST POINT:
850ft (260m) on the valley side

MAPS:
OS Landranger Sheet 115, OS Outdoor Leisure Sheet 17, OS Explorer Sheet 254

REFRESHMENTS:
None: available in Tremadog, to the south-east

ADVICE:
An easy walk, though care is needed near the quarry ruins

A short walk along one of Snowdonia's most beautiful valleys, cradled by high, stark peaks, and drained by a lovely little river.

A   Cwm Pennant

Eifion Wyn, the Welsh shepherd-poet, famously wrote 'O god, why did'st Thou make Cwm Pennant so beautiful, and the life of an old shepherd so short?' Eifion died in 1926 at the age of 59, his life spanning the period when the valley was being exploited for its slate, yet he perceived its beauty. Today the quarrymen have long gone, only the wind disturbing the peace of the upper valley.

Though the above is a statement, Eifion is most famous for his englyns. The englyn is a particular form of Welsh verse consisting of 4 lines with words making up a total of 30 syllables, grouped 10, 6, 7, 7. The first two lines rhyme at the end of 7th and 6th syllables, the last two being a couplet. The verse has no English equivalent as it is based on the sounds of words and is therefore very specific to Welsh. Attempts to translate englyns into English usually fail as they miss much of the point. When heard in Welsh, even if they are not understood, the lyrical quality of the verse seems to mirror the landscape it describes.

The church at Llanfihangel-y-pennant the village at the entrance to Cwm Pennant

The Nantlle Ridge (Mynydd Tal-y-mignedd and Mynydd Drws-y-coed) from Cwm Pennant

a Go through the gate and continue along the road, with the Afon Dwyfor on your left. Where the road turns sharp left to cross the river, continue along the track ahead. Where the track forks, keep left and go through two gates, passing to the right of some farm buildings. When the track takes a sharp hairpin turn to the right, follow the signed bridleway ahead. After about 75 yards (70m), at a waymark post, take the path half-right uphill. Follow the path indicated up the hillside, making for a small copse of conifers. The path soon (at a waymark) turns uphill and zig-zags to reach the right-hand end of the copse. Pass the trees on your left, go through a gate and continue uphill to reach the trackbed of an old tramway.

Cwm Pennant from the start of the walk

B   Slate Quarries

There were several slate quarries high in Cwm Pennant, and the buildings of one of the biggest, the Prince of Wales, at 549 498, are passed on the route. It was connected by tramway to Porthmadog and at its height employed 200 men. Despite significant investment and a production rate which rose to 5,000 tons of stone per year, the quarry remained open for only 13 years, from 1873 to 1886 (though there had been limited, sporadic working at the site as early as 1840). Elsewhere in Cwm Pennant the quarries were small and of limited commercial value, each following a similar pattern to the Prince of Wales, with investment and enthusiastic working followed by a tail off in production and closure.

b   Turn left along the track with breathtaking views of the head wall of the valley. To the right are the lower slopes of Moel Lefn, and to the left the peaks of the Nantlle ridge. Go

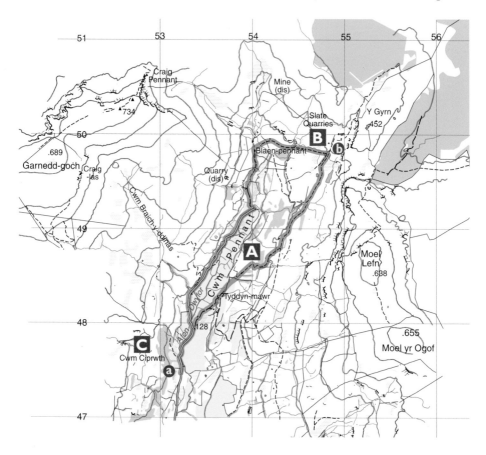

Looking south along the valley from the ruins of the Prince of Wales quarry

through two gates at the old quarry buildings and turn left to go under the central archways of the former dressing shed. Continue straight ahead over the end of old tipped waste and on to the path which skirts around a rocky spur ahead to reach a ladder stile on your left. Cross the stile and follow the waymarked path to the right which leads downhill. At the valley bottom cross a small river by an old stone slab bridge and cross the ladder stile. Continue ahead and then go right along the metalled road to reach the outward route at the bridge over the river.

C Cwm Ciprwth

The valley was once the site of two copper mines, Gilfach and Cwm Ciprwth, whose remains can still be seen. Cwm Pennant also had a third mine, Blaen-y-pennant (also known as Cwmdwyfor) in the high cwm below the Nantlle ridge, at 541 505. None of the mines were very profitable and they were all closed in the late 19th century after just a few decades of production.

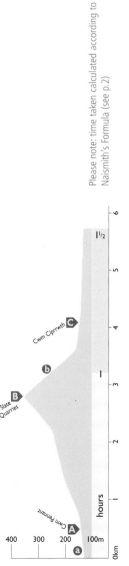

Please note: time taken calculated according to Naismith's Formula (see p.2)

BRYN CADER FANER

START/FINISH:
Trwasfynydd, a village on several bus routes. Drivers can shorten the walk by using a start from verge parking at 685 358

DISTANCE/ASCENT:
12 miles (19km); 5½miles (9km) if the alternative start is used/1,800ft (550m)

APPROXIMATE TIME:
7 hours for the full route, 3½ hours for the short version

HIGHEST POINT:
2,043ft (623m) Moel Ysgyfarnogod

REFRESHMENTS:
Available at Trawsfynydd in summer; taking a picnic is recommended

MAPS:
Harveys Snowdonia South; OS Landranger Sheet 124, OS Outdoor Leisure Sheet 18

ADVICE:
This is tough walk over a rugged, often pathless wilderness. The return walk can be used as an out-and-back alternative to see the stone circle. Unwise to attempt solo; map, compass and protective clothing essential

At the northern end of the Rhinogs, linking the coast (near Harlech) with Llyn Trawsfynydd is a track that has been in use for over 3,000 years. To the south of the track is some of the most exciting, but exacting, walking country in Wales. This is a hard, rugged walk, one for the connoisseur of difficult terrain (which can be very wet after prolonged rain), but also one of the most interesting in central Snowdonia.

A Trawsfynydd

The village name means 'traverse of the mountain' and derives from its position on a road across the high ground between the Mawddach valley and the Vale of Ffestiniog. It is a pleasant village with a statue of its most famous son, the poet Ellis Humphrey Evans, more commonly known by his bardic name Hedd Wyn.

a From the village centre (the car park) walk south down the high street and turn left between the Women's Institute hall and Bodwyn's Café. Left of the playground is a public footpath. Follow this down a lane and through a field to reach a footbridge over the lake.

B Llyn Trawsfynydd

Llyn Trawsfynydd is a natural lake, but was dammed to increase its volume when Maentwrog Hydro-electric Power Station was built in the 1920s. Forty years later the decision to build Trawsfynydd Nuclear Power Station within the National Park was controversial, and to overcome some objections Sir Basil Spence was asked to design the station buildings and Dame Sylvia Crowe landscaped the site. The reactors were of first generation British design, known as Magnox, and fuelled with natural uranium. The station generated 400 MW, but was shut down in the early 1990s and is currently being decommissioned. Lake water still feeds the hydro-electric power station at Maentwrog.

b Turn right along the road staying close to the wall of the lake. Just after the road passes close to the lake, and beyond Tyn Twll Farm on the right, there are two gates on the left. (The alternative start lies close to the gates.) Go through the right-hand gate which is signposted, up a walled path and

Approaching Cwm Moch

then over stiles to reach open, wild country. The aim now is to climb to the summit of Moel Ysgyfarnogod – the hill of the Hares – the highest of the peaks seen from Llyn Trawsfynydd, but behind Diffwys from this point in the route. The toughest way is to fork left and follow the zig-zag path through the heather up Diffwys, skirt the peak of Foel Penolau on its south slope through a gateless wall gap aligned north-west, then follow the wall sharp left to the south-west up a steep grassy hill, and then wind your way up the rocks to the top of Moel Ysgyfarnogod. The peak trig point is the third of four cairns. From the fourth cairn there is an ill-defined track down to Llyn Dywarchen, then pick your way between bog and rocks to Bryn Cader Faner – watch for its coronet shape (this is not apparent until close by and is quite small in size) on its own small knoll in the raised dell. A map and compass are necessary here.

As an alternative to climbing the mountains, the easiest way is to follow the old track down into Cwn Moch, crossing a slab bridge over the stream and following a path uphill before turning southwards to attack the hill.

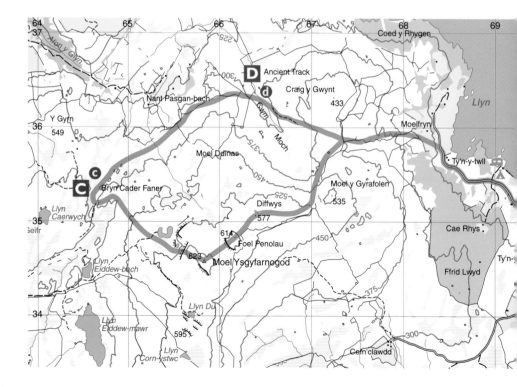

Looking into Cwm Moch from the east

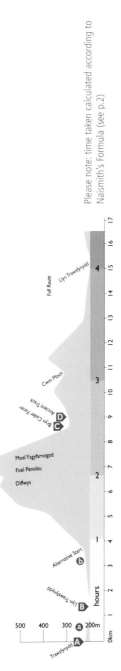

Please note: time taken calculated according to Naismith's Formula (see p.2)

C Bryn Cader Faner 648 353

Until 1940 the Bryn Cader Faner stone circle was the finest Bronze Age site in north Wales, consisting of about 30 stones which, very unusually, leaned outwards rather than standing erect. At the centre of the circle was a burial chamber, the whole being a cairn circle rather than a henge site (as at Stonehenge, to give the very best example). Henge sites (or, at least, some of them) are now speculated to have had astronomical, perhaps predicting the mid-winter or mid-summer solstices, but cairn circles are more likely to have been for ritual purposes relating to the burial at their centre.

Any astronomical significance to the positioning of stones at Bryn Cader Faner is now lost: in 1940 soldiers training in the northern Rhinogs

The stone circle of Bryn Cader Faner has a diameter of 25ft (7.6m) and is 3ft (1m) high

vandalised the circle. Only half the original stones remain, and the position of these cannot be verified against the original plan. Nevertheless the lean of the stone is authentic (from early descriptions) and gives the circle an air of mystery as well as making it look like a discarded giant's crown.

c   From the stone circle head north, downhill, to reach an obvious track heading south-west/north-east. Turn right along the track. The track is occasionally lost in boggy ground – some parts of which it crosses on laid slabs of rock – but maintains a north-easterly direction to reach a wall: continue more easily now with the wall on your left. Cross a stile and continue to cross a slab bridge and another stile. The route now descends into Cwm Moch.

D   The Ancient Track
The track through Cwm Moch links the coast near Harlech with Llyn Trawsfynydd. It is an ancient route, the standing stones beside it and Bryn Cader Faner, implying a usage from at least the Bronze Age: as now Bronze Age folk built beside the road. Later peoples also used the road: to the south-west of Bryn Cader Faner, Moel Goedog is topped by an Iron Age hillfort, perhaps defending the route. There are also hut circles close by.

Later again, in medieval times, the route was used by drovers, a practice which continued until the 19th century. In the days before refrigeration the drovers delivered meat on the hoof ready for slaughter in town. Wales is crossed by a large number of such roads – there is another across the southern Rhinogs – the sheep and cattle farmers of the country delivering their meat to the towns of England. A drove would have been a fine sight, as not only sheep and cows were driven, but pigs and goats, and even poultry – chickens, geese and turkeys. Poultry sometimes had their feet encased in pitch so that they could withstand the rigours of the walk. Bulls were also shod for the walk, the blacksmiths who carried out the shoeing being both very skilled and very, very brave.

d Cross the slab bridge in Cwm Moch and ascend to reach the outward route. Now reverse the outward route to regain the start.

An ancient clapper bridge over the stream in Cwm Moch

THE ROMAN STEPS

START/FINISH:
At 647 314, the car park at the eastern end of Llyn Cwm Bychan. This point is not reached by public transport

DISTANCE/ASCENT:
6 miles (9.5km)/2,000ft (600m)

APPROXIMATE TIME:
3–4 hours

HIGHEST POINT:
2,362ft (720m) Rhinog Fawr

MAPS:
Harveys Snowdonia South; OS Landranger Sheet 124, OS Outdoor Leisure Sheet 18

REFRESHMENTS:
None on the route: available in Llanbedr to the west

ADVICE:
The outward route is well trodden and Rhinog Fawr is a good landmark. The return route is often pathless moor. Compass skills are needed

This fine route starts from one of Snowdonia's most beautiful valleys, climbs the most impressive, but not the highest of the Rhinogs and ascends ancient steps whose origin is still the cause of debate.

A Cwm Bychan
The starting car park for this route is reached by a drive through this exquisite valley. The car park itself is close to the valley's lake, a lovely stretch of water with surprising tree cover for so wild a spot.

a Go through the gate at the top of the car park follow the obvious, well-trodden path south towards Rhinog Fawr. Go through a good stretch of woodland, exiting over a ladder stile. Cross another stile and a tiny hump-back bridge. Continue for 275 yards (250m) or so to reach a path going off right, by a stone slab bridging a small stream: this is the return route. Take the left-hand fork to reach the Roman Steps.

B The Roman Steps
The age of the steps has been debated for many years and though a consensus view has been reached, there are still some who disagree. It is likely that the pass of Bwlch Tyddiad was in use in prehistoric times, and equally likely that the Romans did indeed use the route, and probably improved it by adding stone slabs. But the spacing of the present slabs suggest they were placed for use by packhorses and are, therefore, likely to be medieval in origin.

Rhinog Fawr seen across Gloyw Lyn

The Roman Steps

b Occasionally the steps disappear, but the route is always obvious. Go through a gate and continue up the steps. As the pass (Bwlch Tyddiad) narrows continue to a crossing wall at 657 301. Turn right and follow a path beside the wall steeply uphill to reach a point above Llyn Du. The return route crosses the wall here – there is a stone stile – but not before Rhinog Fawr has been climbed. Head in a southerly direction to reach a ladder stile at 652 287. Do not cross this stile, instead follow the good path that heads north-east to the top of Rhinog Fawr. The view southward from here, across Bwlch Drws-Ardudwy to Rhinog Fach is excellent.

Sunset over Llyn Cwm Bychan

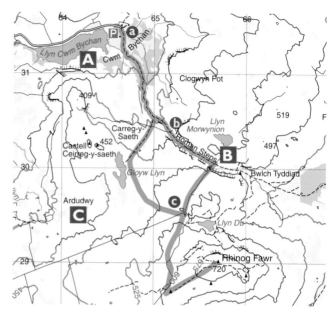

C Ardudwy

In medieval times Ardudwy, the coastal plain between the
Rhinogs and the sea, was the home of a band of outlaws who
used the great wall of the Rhinog peaks as protection. Using
their knowledge of the secret ways through the peaks they
raided the lands to the east, stealing cattle and other goods
and then returning to Ardudwy. On one trip into Clwyd they
kidnapped several women from a village. The Clwyd menfolk
were outraged, and of much sterner stuff than any the
Ardudwy bandits had troubled before. A gang was formed and
they found the Bwlch Tyddiad route through the Rhinogs,
surprising the bandits and killing many of them. The rescued
women were brought back through the pass, but in their time
as captives of the bandits they had fallen in love with them
and, anguished by their deaths and appalled at the prospects
of a return to their old lives in Clwyd, they threw themselves
into a lake beside the pass and drowned. The lake is Llyn
Morwynion, the Lake of Maidens, though the word 'maiden'
seems hardly appropriate in view of the story.

c   Retrace your steps down Rhinog Fawr and return to the
wall above Llyn Du and cross the stile. Please note that where
the path forks take the track to the right leading down a little
gully, this will take you direct to the stone stile level with Llyn
Du. Follow the path beyond north-westward. Soon Gloyw Llyn
comes into view. Caution is needed now. Below you there is a

The tiny humpback bridge crossed twice on the walk

loose pile of boulders. Follow the indistinct path as it bears left to reach the far side of a gully and then follows the left (as viewed) side of the gully downwards. At the bottom, bear right across boggy ground to reach a terrace above Gloyw Llyn. Now bear right, maintaining your distance from, and height above the lake. The path is occasionally indistinct, but is better beyond a ruined sheepfold. Go over a ladder stile in a wall and follow the now distinct path to reach the outward route. Turn left, soon reaching the little humpbacked bridge. Now follow the outward route back to the start.

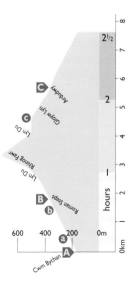

Y LLETHR AND RHINOG FACH

START/FINISH:
Verge parking is available near the end of the road in Cwm Nantcol (640 268), but it is more considerate to pay the small fee to park in the car park at the end of the road near Maes-y-Garnedd (642 270). This point is not reached by public transport

DISTANCE/ASCENT:
9½ miles (15km)/2,600ft (800m)

APPROXIMATE TIME:
6 hours

HIGHEST POINT:
2,480ft (756m) Y Llethr

MAPS:
Harveys Snowdonia South; OS Landranger Sheet 124, OS Outdoor Leisure Sheet 18 (recommended)

REFRESHMENTS:
None on the route: available in Llanbedr, to the west

ADVICE:
An easy-to-follow route, but with a stiff climb to Rhinog Fach. A map, compass and protective clothing are advised. Do not attempt the walk in poor visibility

Though the central Rhinogs are dominated by the two peaks which name the range – Rhinog Fawr and Rhinog Fach – these are not the highest summits. To the south of the Rhinog Fach, both Y Llethr and Diffwys are higher, Y Llethr being the highest of the range's peaks. As a summit Y Llethr is disappointing, but the walk to it from Rhinog Fach is one of the most spectacular in this area of the National Park.

A Cwm Nantcol

The starting point for this walk is one of the most remote of any in the National Park, but does have the advantage of a drive along Cwm Nantcol. As with nearby Cwm Bychan (see Walk 19), this is a delightful valley. Four miles (6.5km) from the start is the Salem Baptist Chapel, made famous by the painting of Curnow Vosper. The painting is of the congregation of the chapel (who were each paid 6d – the old sixpence – in 1910 to sit for Vosper who painted the work 'live'). The central character is Shani Owen, and in the folds of her shawl many see the face of the devil, though it has never been definitely established that this was Vosper's intention or

Cwm Nantcol and the gateposts
of Rhinog Fawr and Rhinog Fach

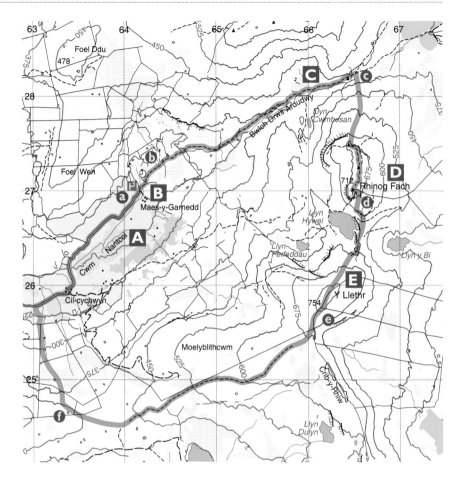

whether it was an accident. Expert opinion favours the former, Vosper wanting to illustrate the hypocrisy of folk who were regular chapel goers, but could not always be regarded as Christians. Shani Owen does seem to exemplify this, her stance and face seemingly set to express her piety, yet doing a much better job of conveying the idea that she was not a lady to cross or to be sympathetic towards ideas which differed from her own.

Beyond Salem there is a car park from which a signed nature trail explores the woodland of the southern edge of Nantcol, visiting a fine waterfall.

a Walk to the end of the road, reaching Maes-y-Garnedd (where the parking fee should be paid).

B Maes-y-Garnedd 642 269

Maes-y-Garnedd was the birthplace of John Jones, an ardent Parliamentarian during the Civil War. Jones, who was disliked by his neighbours for both his beliefs – most were Royalist sympathisers – and for his arrogance, rose quickly through the ranks of Cromwell's army. He was eventually made a colonel, though being, by then, Cromwell's brother-in-law (having married Catherine Cromwell) may have had some part in his advancement. As Col John Jones he was appointed to the panel of judges who sentenced Charles I to death. At the restoration 29 of the judges were sentenced to death for regicide. Nineteen were reprieved, but Jones and nine others suffered the traitor's execution of hanging, drawing and quartering. After the butchering Jones' remains were, as usual, placed on public display, in part for approval, in part as a deterrence. Samuel Pepys, in his famous diary, notes that one day as he was out walking the 'steaming remains' of Jones were carted past him on their way to their display point.

b From the house, take the obvious, signed path heading north-east towards the even more obvious pass of Bwlch Drws Ardudwy, the pass between the prominent peaks of Rhinog Fawr (to the left – north) and Rhinog Fach. The path follows a wall, on the right, at first, then continues in straightforward, if rugged, fashion into the pass. There are several options for ascending Rhinog Fach, paths heading off towards it as the pass path rises: ignore these, following the path through the pass which broadens at a point almost due south of Rhinog Fawr, then tightens again. At the top of the pass there is a prominent cairn.

C Bwlch Drws Ardudwy

Bwlch Drws Ardudwy is the Pass of the Door of Ardudwy, the door standing between the rhinogau, doorposts, of Rhinog Fawr and Rhinog Fach. It is these 'doorposts' which name the range. The pass linked the coastal plain of Ardudwy, famous for its prehistoric sites (especially at Dyffryn Ardudwy to the south of Llanbedr, from which Cwm Nantcol heads east) and as the homeground of the men of Ardudwy, the famous band of outlaws (see Note to Walk 19). Thomas Pennant, the late 18th century traveller, described his visit to the pass in his book Tour in Wales. He 'found the horror of it far exceeding the most gloomy idea that could be conceived of it'. It is strange that the wildness that so horrified Pennant is now the reason why walkers seek out the pass. But equally odd is Pennant's reaction: did he really find the pass horrifying? Eighteenth century travel writing is full of such comments,

Please note: time taken calculated according to Naismith's Formula (see p.2)

folk pulling down the blinds on coach windows so as to avoid
the horrors of mountainscapes, and other similar incidents.
Have our sensitivities changed that much?, or was it a 'fad' of
the time, like women swooning?

c   Continue on the path to a gap in the wall, go through it,
then turn right and walk beside the wall down to a wall ahead.
Cross this where it has collapsed and follow a distinct, but
steep path up the rugged face of Rhinog Fach. Walk along the
ridge to the summit cairn.

D   Rhinog Fach 666 272

During steps to catch your breath on the ascent, look out for
clumps of mossy saxifrage, with its long leafy shoots and
delicate white flowers. The acidic Rhinogs are not renowned
for their plant life, mossy saxifrage being one of few flowers
to be found among the heather.

d   Near the cairn a wall running in from the west comes to
an end. Walk west keeping the wall on your left. Do not
continue to the corner but cut across a jumble of rock to join
the wall going south. There is no clearly discernible path but
a slight brownish tinge on the rocks indicates the way most
people have chosen to go. Continue downhill with care as the
way is steep and rocky, still keeping the wall on the left. At the
bottom the col between Rhinog Fach and Y Llethr is reached
with steep slabs falling away to your right into Llyn Hywel.
Start the ascent by keeping close to the wall, but where an
obvious path veers away to the right follow it. Before long the
path seems to peter out, but a steep eroded path of loose
stones appears up on the left heading back towards the wall
which cannot be seen at this point. After a stiff climb the wall
is rejoined. Continue uphill (still with the wall on the left),
until a flat grassy area is reached. A cairn on the right marks
the summit.

E   Y Llethr 661 258

Y Llethr just means 'the slope', a reference to the ice-
smoothed slabs rising from Llyn Hywel (Howell's Lake), the
lake formed in the glacial hollow enclosed by Y Llethr and
Rhinog Fach. Interestingly the hollow contains two lakes
rather than the more normal one, indicating a small side
glacier or the main glacier splitting around the ridge of rock
which separates the two. Llyn Perfeddau is a lovely little lake,
but the name does not reflect its perfection: the names means
Lake of Entrails – does it derive from local satisfaction with
the death (and its method) of John Jones?

e From the summit walk downhill towards two ladder stiles; ignore the one to the left and cross the one in the wall ahead. Turn right and walk beside the wall descending the broad ridge of Moelyblithcwm. When the wall turns sharp right head for the elbow of another wall about ¾ mile (1.2km) away. Follow the wall (it should be on your right) to reach a ladder stile with an adjacent gate. From here to the left a path leads down to Pont Scethin, one of the most unlikely, yet romantically-sited bridges in Wales. Walkers exploring the Ysgethin valley to the west of Diffwys for the first time are frequently amazed to discover that it was once crossed by the coach road to Harlech, a route that must have been an epic journey.

f Cross the ladder stile and follow a path that heads just west of north, descending towards Cwm Nantcol. The path goes through two old walls and then a gate. Continue through pasture land until the unfenced road is reached. Turn right and follow the road back to the start.

Llyn Hywel and Y Llethr from Rhinog Fach

RIVER MAWDDACH

START/FINISH:
At 696 185, the car park
beside the RSPB Observatory
at Penmaenpool. Penmaenpool
is a stop on the Crosville bus
that links Dolgellau and Tywyn

DISTANCE/ASCENT:
5 miles (8km)/800ft (250m)

APPROXIMATE TIME:
2½ hours

HIGHEST POINT:
800ft (250m) On the slopes on
Dolgledr

MAPS:
OS Landranger Sheet 124, OS
Outdoor Leisure Sheet 18

REFRESHMENTS:
The George III Hotel has one of
the best restaurants in the
area. Dolgellau and Barmouth
also have a full range of
possibilities

ADVICE:
Easy walking, partly on the
trackbed of an old railway;
contains some moderate
ascents

The Dyfi and Mawddach rivers are the finest in Snowdonia.
This short walk follows part of a trail that explores the
estuarine section of the Mawddach, a haven for birds.

A Penmaenpool

The Mawddach is a beautiful river, rising on the rarely visited
uplands between the A470 and Llyn Tegid (Bala Lake). It
flows through the Coed-y-Brenin, the King's Forest, where
Rhaedr Mawddach is one of Snowdonia's prettiest waterfalls.
West of Dolgellau, and especially near Penmaenpool, the
Mawddach estuary is famous for its bird life. As would be
expected, waders are the main residents and migrants, but
redshanks, oystercatchers, curlew, little grebes, water rails
and red-breasted mergansers are seen all year. The area is
also excellent for warblers in summer. In winter there is
usually a resident peregrine falcon. The RSPB Observatory,
housed in the signal box of the old railway, has information on
the bird species the walker might see, and a list of the birds
which have be seen recently.

Because of its beauty the Mawddach has always been popular
with poets. John Ruskin wrote that the only walk in Britain
which was finer than that from Dolgellau to Barmouth was the
walk from Barmouth to Dolgellau. Gerald Manley Hopkins
also loved the river. Penmaenpool was his favourite spot and
featured in one of his verses:

The Mawddach estuary

Who long for rest, who look for pleasure
Away from counter, court or school
O where live well your lease of leisure
But here, here at Penmaenpool.

The Mawddach and the George
III hotel from the start of the
walk

a From the car park, turn right along the main road (the
A493), then cross, with care, to turn sharp left along a signed
path. Follow the path uphill, keeping to the left of a large new
house, through excellent woodland – where the sharp eyed
will see blackcaps, wood warblers and other smaller birds –
to reach a gate. Turn left along a track with yellow
waymarkers, bearing right at a fork to continue following the
yellow waymarkers uphill through the wood. At a pond, turn
right along a path (still following the waymarkers), going
steeply uphill to reach steps and a ladder stile out of the
woodland. There is a magnificent view of Cadair Idris from
here, best seen in the winter when the trees are not in leaf.
Walk straight ahead until a track is reached.

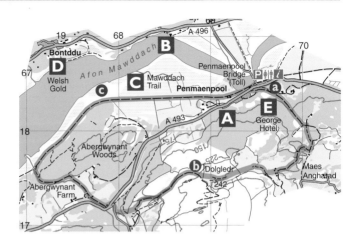

Turn right onto the track, but where it bears right, maintain direction towards a house, going through gates to pass it. Turn right through a field (wall on left), to rejoin a track, cross two ladder stiles and continue to a farm. Now turn right to reach a waymarked gate. Go through and turn half left, uphill, to reach a waymarker post. Turn right and follow a track to a gate and ladder stile. Cross the stile and a small stream. Bear left through a gap in a wall and continue uphill (fence, then wall, on left) towards another ladder stile over a wall ahead. Cross the stile. A broad, level grassy track leads on and there are several tracks leading up to a ridge. Take the furthest of these which has a post visible at the top (weather permitting). From the ridge there is a magnificent view of the Mawddach estuary.

The old railway signal box, now an RSPB observatory and information centre

B   Mawddach Estuary

The point where the Mawddach reaches the sea is a busy place. To the north is Barmouth a Victorian seaside resort once favoured by Charles Darwin and the poets Wordsworth, Shelley and Tennyson. Before it was a resort it had been a port, its principal export a coarse woollen cloth produced by local cottage weavers. Conditions for the weavers were miserable, a grim story of exploitation by (usually English) merchants. In a tale of circular cause and effect which would be almost laughable if it were not so terrible, the coarse cloth of the exploited Welsh weavers was used to clothe the even more exploited black slaves of American cotton plantations, the cotton providing cheap clothing in Britain which had caused the decline of the English woollen industry and led to its closure and misery for English weavers.

The river mouth is crossed by a wooden viaduct built in 1860 and now carrying the Cambrian Coast railway. It is also a toll bridge for walkers. On the southern side of the bridge, at Fairbourne, another of the 'Great Little Trains of Wales' follows a crooked finger of land poked out into the estuary so far it almost scratches the nose of Barmouth.

Legend has it that to the west of the estuary, in Barmouth Bay, there was once a fertile piece of land called Cantref Gwaelod, protected from the sea by a huge wall. The land was ruled by a king who neglected the wall, entrusting its maintenance and repair to men who should not have been trusted. The king's son, Prince Elffin, concerned for the land's safety when a huge storm threatened the bay, warned the people to move to higher land, a warning that saved many lives when the sea wall collapsed and Gwaelod was engulfed. Returning to survey the damage after the storm had abated, Elffin realised his homeland had gone forever, but his despair was tempered by the discovery of a baby boy saved from drowning by being caught in a salmon trap. Elffin raised the boy and he became Taliesin, the famous Celtic bard whose memorial is seen on Walk 8.

b   Turn half left to the ladder stile in the angle of the wall and cross it. Turn right along a track and follow it downhill crossing two more ladder stiles. Go through a gate on to a minor road, turn right and continue to the A493. Turn left, but soon cross with care and turn right along the drive leading to Abergwynant Farm where the track turns left to cross the bridge, and continue to the farm. Follow the track ahead with the Afon Gwynant on your left. Go through two gates and into

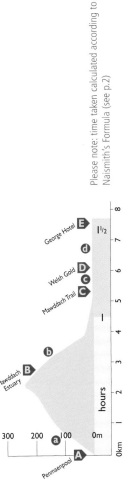

the Abergwynant Woods. Follow the woodland track as it bears left, but where it bears right maintain direction to reach a waymarked post. Continue ahead, go through a gate and up to the trackbed of an old railway.

C The Mawddach Trail
The railway once linked Barmouth Junction (now Morfa Mawddach Station) to Dolgellau, joining the Cambrian Coast line to the Vale of Dee line. It opened in 1868 and closed in 1965. It carried passengers to the coastal resort of Barmouth, but also transported slate and copper from local quarries and mines. The trackbed now forms the Mawddach Trail, a fine 9½ mile (12km) walk.

c The village of Bontddu is visible on the far side of the river. Turn right and continue along the track bed to regain the car park at Penmaenpool.

D   Welsh Gold

Above Bontddu is the Clogau gold mine. Gold was discovered in Wales in the 1830s by prospectors looking for copper. The mines are confined to a triangle linking Trawsfynydd, Bala and Barmouth and are famed for producing a gold which is slightly paler than usual. By tradition, the wedding rings of the British royal family are made of Welsh gold. From this section of the Mawddach Trail there is a fine view of the Arans.

E   The George Hotel

The hotel was built in the mid-17th century and, externally, has been little altered. At one time a section of the hotel was used as an inn for men building the railway and workers on the Penmaen Uchaf Estate.

The toll bridge beside the hotel was built in 1879 and at that time could be opened to allow the passage of sailing ships.

Penmaenpool and the woodland of Ffridd y Mynydd from across the Mawddach

CADAIR IDRIS: THE FOX'S AND PONY PATHS

START/FINISH:
The car park at 698 153 on the minor road from Dolgellau. There is no public transport to this point

DISTANCE/ASCENT:
9 miles (14.5km)/2,500ft (750m)

APPROXIMATE TIME:
6 hours

HIGHEST POINT:
2,929ft (893m) Pen y Gadair

MAPS:
OS Landranger Sheet 124, OS Outdoor Leisure Sheet 23

REFRESHMENTS:
The Gwernan Lake Hotel. There is also a wide range of opportunities in Dolgellau.

ADVICE:
The descent of the Fox's Path should be avoided, and care should be taken not to stray too close to the huge Cyfrwy cliffs. This is a strenuous walk over rugged, wet terrain so suitable clothing should be worn. Do not attempt this walk in bad weather

From the north Cadair Idris is a huge wall of mountain, as impressive as any range in the National Park. This route attacks this northern flank finding an easy way up to the highest peak.

A   Cadair Idris

Cadair Idris means the Chair of Idris. The chair can be seen in either Cwm Gadair or Cwm Cau as each has a fine back and equally good armrests. But if two options seem one too many, it is a small number in comparison to the number of candidates for Idris. Many of the past writers on the range have noted simply that Idris was a local giant, but that is avoiding the issue as Wales is full of 'local giants' and there are, in any case, no stories of giants specific to these hills, or any other giant associations – standing stones, mounds of earth etc.

Another story links the range with Idris ap Gwyddno, a Celtic prince who died in a battle against encroaching Saxons or Irish in the early 7th century. Idris was certainly a real man, but the battle is referred to as the 'slaughter of the Severn' as it took place near the river's source on Plynlimon, surely too far away to be a realistic reason for naming Cadair after him.

Finally it is occasionally suggested that Idris was a Celtic poet who used the peak for meditation. One combination of legends maintains that the poet Idris Garw was also a giant who used the chair to seek inspiration from gazing at the night sky. There is a local saying, probably deriving from this

Llyn y Gadair and Cyfrwy from Pen y Gadair with, beyond, the Mawddach estuary and Barmouth

association, that anyone who spends a night on the peak will, in the morning, be either a poet or a madman. But this saying is by no means specific to Cadair Idris, being associated with several other locations in Wales.

a From the car park, return to the road and turn right, following it for a few yards to reach a signed track, on the left, by the telephone box. This is the Pony Path.

B The Pony Path

The Pony Path is the old trackway across Cadair Idris, linking Llanfihangel-y-Pennant (and the Dysynni Valley beyond) to the Mawddach Valley and Dolgellau. Llanfihangel-y-Pennant is famous as the home of Mary Jones who, in 1800 at the age of 16, walked barefoot to Bala – a distance of 25 miles (40km) – to buy a Bible in Welsh from Thomas Charles the town's vicar. Rev Charles had sold the last of his stock, but was so impressed by Mary's determination and fortitude that he gave her his own copy, and, soon after, founded the British and Foreign Bible Society. Close to the village is Castell-y-Bere,

Cadair Idris viewed from Llynnau Cregennen to the west

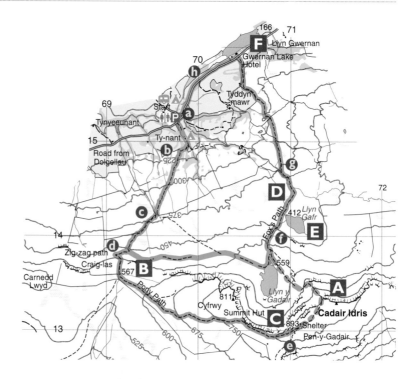

once the fortress of the Princes of Gwynedd. In the 19th century after the Victorians had discovered the Welsh mountains, Cadair Idris became a popular destination. Many of the visitors were unused to walking, and not too keen on the idea either, and hired ponies as well as guides to be taken up the peak. The track's name seems to derive from this era rather than its earlier use as a packhorse trail.

b Follow the track to Ty Nant Farm, going through a kissing gate and then crossing a concrete bridge. Now follow the waymarked path through beautiful woodland – there is hazel, sycamore, ash and birch here, as well as hawthorn bushes – to reach open country, climbing to reach the second of two gates in a wall. From here (696 143) a path leads off east towards Llyn y Gadair. This path is not taken now but we return to it later in the walk.

c Continue along the pony path ahead, occasionally climbing slabs of slate placed to counteract the erosion of countless feet.

d Finally the path uses constructed zig-zags to reach the col between Craig-las, to the right, and Pen y Gadair, to the left. Follow the well-worn path left which heads away from the cliffs of Cyfrwy, taking the southern flank of the broad Pen y Gadair ridge. Eventually the path returns to the cliff edge, allowing a superb view of Llyn y Gadair: continue up the ridge to the summit with its shelter.

C Summit Hut 711 131

The hut at the summit of Pen y Gadair replaces a much older one from which a very old lady would serve tea to the 19th century visitors. The old lady beat them all to the summit, rising very early and trekking to the peak with supplies of firewood, water, tea, milk and sugar. One the tourists who visited the summit was Charles Darwin. He thought the peak 'a grand fellow' though it is not recorded whether Darwin bought the old lady's tea.

e The obvious return route for a superb circular walk is to descend the Fox's Path which ascends the clear broad gully to the north-east of Pen y Gadair. Sadly the path, up a steep scree slope, is badly eroded and very hazardous in descent. Those determined to descend the path will have no difficulty in finding it. More sensible walkers should return to the col between Craig-las and Pen y Gadair, perhaps taking a line closer to the Cyfrwy clefts to improve the view. Now descend the zig-zag path. Near the bottom (back at d) by the remains of a wire fence take an indistinct path to the right which traverses below the Cyfrwy cliffs. This path sometimes peters out going through boggy sections. If you aim to walk between the cliffs and a hillock on your left-hand side you will eventually (702 138) pick up the path which takes you around the hillock to join the lower path going off described at the end of para b. Turn right and ascend this path, keeping the scree to the right, to reach Llyn Y Gadair's north-west corner. Go round the lake's northern tip to reach Fox's path.

D Fox's Path

The Fox's Path is said to have been named because Victorian visitors frequently saw foxes while descending the track. In 1823 a gold torc (necklace) dating from the first millennium BC and made in Ireland was found beside the path. The torc was 42in (107cm) long and weighed ½ lb (225g).

From the point at which the route joins the Fox's Path, the view south, across Llyn y Gadair, to the steep cliffs of Cyfrwy and Pen y Gadair is one of the finest in Wales.

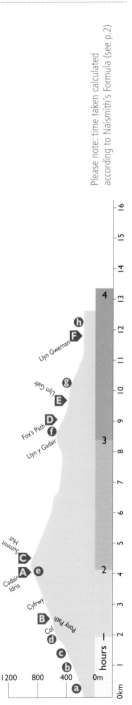

Please note: time taken calculated according to Naismith's Formula (see p.2)

f Turn left along the Fox's path. The path is magnificent: it is a tragedy that its final section has been so marred by erosion.

E Llyn Gafr 711 141

Llyn Gafr is Goat Lake, a lovely little lake in which water lobelia and rushes thrive. Close to the lake, look out for eyebright and golden-rod. The area is also popular with wheatears.

g Cross the outflow stream from Llyn Gafr – a lot easier to accomplish in dry weather than after sustained rain – and descend through superb country with the Rhinogs dominating the view ahead. The path is always obvious and so good that the road near Llyn Gwernan and the Gwernan Lake Hotel is reached almost with regret.

F   Llyn Gwernan 705 160
Beautiful, reed-fringed Llyn Gwernan is said to be the home of a malevolent water spirit who cast spells over locals, causing them to rush into the lake and drown. Few ever came into contact with the spirit and survived, but one local, walking past the lake in the late evening, clearly heard the spirit call out 'The hour is come, but the man is not'. Fearing his safety the man hurried on, but was shortly passed by frenzied, half-dressed man who rushed past him and plunged into the water.

g   Turn left and follow the road for about ⅔ mile (1km) to return to the start.

Cadair Idris from the start of the walk

CADAIR IDRIS: THE MINFFORDD PATH

This route involves more climbing than that on the northern side of the hill, but compensates with a visit to one of the most picturesque mountain hollows in Snowdonia.

START/FINISH:
The car park at 732 116, off the B4405 close to its junction with the A487. There are several buses which stop at this point on a route from Aberystwyth to Porthmadog via Dolgellau

DISTANCE/ASCENT:
7 miles (11km)/3,300ft (1000m) total of three ascents

APPROXIMATE TIME:
5½ hours

HIGHEST POINT:
2,929ft (893m) Pen y Gadair

MAPS:
OS Landranger Sheet 124, OS Outdoor Leisure Sheet 23

REFRESHMENTS:
None nearby: available at Corris to the south

ADVICE:
A straightforward, but strenuous walk over wet, boggy country so suitable clothing should be worn. Do not attempt in adverse weather conditions. Care should be taken not to stray to close to the huge cliffs of Craig Cau

A Tal-y-llyn Lake

The lake (Llyn Myngil in Welsh) differs from virtually all the lakes passed on routes described in this book in not being glacial in origin. It was formed when a landslide into the valley of the Afon Dysynni formed a natural dam at what is now the lake's south-western tip. The lake has given its name to another of Wales' 'Great Little Trains', this one linking Abergynolwyn, to the south-west of the lake, to Tywyn on the coast of Cardigan Bay. The line passes close to Craig yr Aderyn, Bird Rock, on which cormorants nest, several miles from the sea.

a   There are two routes from the car park. It is possible to go through the gate at the far end of the car park and following a raised causeway along an avenue of chestnut trees. Go past the CCW Visitor Centre to reach a gate into the National Nature Reserve oak wood. Better is to return to the road and to turn right (towards Tal-y-llyn Lake: although the lake is not passed by the route it is seen to perfection on the return). After a short distance the gates of the old Idris estate are reached on the right. Go through and follow the old drive past rhododendron bushes and along an avenue of Scots pine. This way, the regal entrance to the Minffordd Estate seems a more fitting way to start the Path which bears the estate's name. Go through the gate into the Nature Reserve.

Llyn Cau and Craig Cau from Pen y Gadair. The route follows the Craig Cau ridge

B Cadair Idris National Nature Reserve

The Reserve covers Cwm Cau, the cliffs above it (which form the 'wall' of Craig Cau, Pen y Gadair and Mynydd Moel) and the wooded slopes of Ystrad Gwyn up which the Minffordd Path rises. The oak wood here is believed to date from the end of the last Ice Age – that means it has been here for about 8,000 years. Fences protect this remarkable survival from grazing, but higher up, as elsewhere, the accessible slopes have been grazed by sheep and now support little apart from heather and sheep's fescue, though there are also patches of bilberry. The steeper sections of cliff, where the sheep cannot reach, are home to rarer species such as the pink tuffs of wild angelica, purple saxifrage, Devil's-bit scabious, moss campion and dwarf willow, as well as ferns such as alpine and lesser meadowrue, and green spleenwort. The cliffs are also the southern limit of mountain sorrel and lesser clubmoss. There is also a small population of hairy greenwood, an extraordinary survival as elsewhere in Britain this rare plant grows only in sheltered and sunny lowland sites. Finally, there are patches of the rare and easily overlooked stiff sedge.

Of bird life, as elsewhere, the uplands have breeding pairs of ravens and ring ouzels, and walkers will occasionally be treated to the sight of a red kite. The kite's breeding range is now expanding quickly from its former last stronghold of mid-

Cwm Cau – Pen y Gadair across the lake

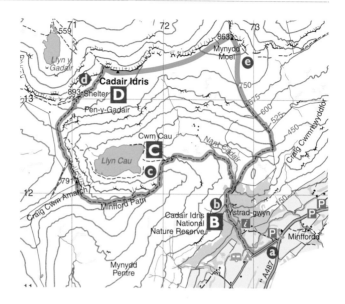

Wales and birds are often seen at the RSPB Reserve at Ynyshir, just across the Dyfi, and above the surrounding hills.

b Follow the path close to the Nant Cadair stream, climbing steeply through woodland, sometimes on wooden steps placed to limit further erosion. Exit the woodland through a gate and continue along the well-trodden path to reach Cwm Cau. At the path fork the route follows the left-hand branch: the right-hand branch continues to Llyn Cau.

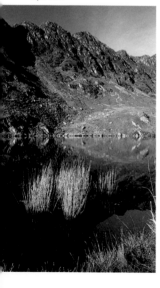

Llyn Cau

C Cwm Cau

Cwm Cau is an almost perfect glacial corrie – indeed, it is often quoted in geography/geology textbooks as the example of the type. But with its steep, ice-plucked cliffs towering above dark Llyn Cau, it is also one of the most beautiful cwms in Britain. Cwm Cau, and Cwm Gadair on the northern side of the high ridge, have long been a favourite with poets, the bard Gwilym Cowlyd (1827-1905) writing a famous englyn to the lakes.

> Y llynnau gwyrddion llonydd – a gysgant
> Mewn gwasgod o fynydd;
> A thynn heulwen ysblennydd
> Ar len y dwr lun y dydd

which translates as 'The calm green lakes are sleeping in the mountain shadow, and on the water's canvas bright sunshine paints the picture of the day'.

c Follow the left-hand path, climbing steeply. Continue on the winding path marked by cairns eventually reaching a ladder stile at the top of Craig Cau. Cross the stile and descend along the cliff edge (with marvellous views of the cwm) into Bwlch Cau. The path now climbs steeply to reach the summit and shelter of Pen y Gadair.

d Now head north-east, with excellent views down into Cwm Gadair, particularly from the top of the Fox's Path, following the cliff edge (on the left) to reach the summit of Mynydd Moel. The view northwards over the Mawddach estuary to the Rhinogs is superb.

D Cadair Idris

The slopes of Cadair Idris are said to be the haunt of Gwyn ap Nudd who led his Cwn Annwfn (Hounds of the Underworld) in search of the souls of the dead. The howling of the dogs – huge, white animals with red ears – foretold death to anyone who heard them, their souls joining those of the recently departed in being swept up by the pack and herded to the Underworld.

e Cross a ladder stile and descend south-eastwards beside a fence, with an opening view into Cwm Cau to the right. Descend past two ladder stiles keeping the fence to your right until you reach a third ladder stile at the bottom of a newly worked path. This is a very steep section but there are fine views of Tallyllyn lake on your right. Cross the stile, follow the path, crossing the Nant Cadair stream – a lot easier to accomplish in dry weather than after sustained rain – to regain the outward path near the woodland exit gate. Now reverse the outward route back to the start.

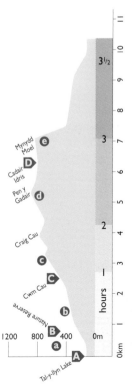

Please note: time taken calculated according to Naismith's Formula (see p.2)

BWLCH OERDDRWS AND WAUN OER

To the south of the A470 as it bends its way steeply up towards Bwlch Oerddrws are some of the least visited peaks in the Snowdonia Nation Park. The confirmed hillwalker may find the long undulating ridges a little tame, but for newcomers to the Welsh mountains there are few better places to start, with a short steady climb to an incomparable viewpoint.

A Bwlch Oerddrws

Bwlch Oerddrws is the Pass of the Cold Door, probably named for the winds which spill chillingly through it in winter. Until the 13th century the upper Dyfi Valley and the side valleys of the Afon Cerist, the Afon Cywarch (visited on Walk 25) and the Afon Dugoed, were a small kingdom, peopled by red-haired folk who were fiercely independent. But Llywelyn ap Iorwerth (Llywelyn the Great) had no interest in such enclaves – they spoiled the continuity of his princedom. He forced open the cold door and made the valley folk to swear allegiance to him. This they did, grudgingly, but their geographical isolation allowed them to continue much as before. By the late 17th century they had begun to raid the more prosperous folk of the surrounding area whose wealth had increased while their own valleys' economics had stagnated. Soon the red-haired bandits of the hidden valleys had become a considerable menace to the law-abiding peoples of what is now southern Gwynedd and northern Powys.

Cribin Fawr from the Cerist Valley below Bwlch Oerddrws

Finally on Christmas Eve of a year in the early 18th century, a local baron took an armed bunch of men into the valley, capturing almost 100 bandits. He hauled them out of the valley, condemning many of them to death for their past crimes. Two of those condemned were very young and their mother pleaded with the baron, claiming they had never been bandits, not being old enough for such things. The baron refused her plea, and the execution was carried out. The mother then cursed the baron, telling him that her family would one day wash their hands in the baron's blood. Soon after, the baron and his son were attacked and stabbed to death at a place still known as Llidiart-y-barwn, the Baron's Gate.

But any joy the mother felt at this retribution was short-lived. The baron's successor invaded the valley, killing more red-

Waun Oer from Cribin Fawr. In the distance is Cadair Idris

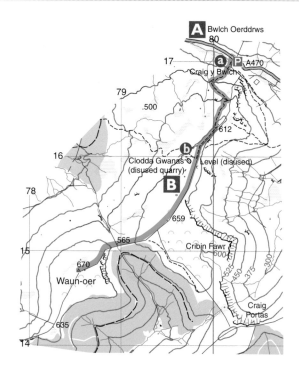

haired folk and imposing tight control on the remainder. Today only the memory of the bandits lives on – in the name of the Brigands Inn at Mallwyd and in the sign of the famous Meirion Mill at Dinas Mawddwy.

a From the lay-by car park, go over the ladder stile and follow the fence line towards the bottom of the mountainside. Where the fence turns sharp left, bear right to follow a faint grassy path uphill. Later on this path is not always clearly discernible on the ground, particularly on the rocky sections. Keep looking up to check if you can see the line of the path ahead and refer to the map with care.

B Gloddfa Gwanas Quarry 798 160

Information on the quarry is scant, but it seems to have been worked only sporadically. Originally the slate was hauled away by packhorse – along a route heading westwards – bur later a rudimentary tramway was constructed. The slate produced was of relatively poor quality. This, together with the difficulties of transport and the never ending battle with the elements – the quarry being above the 2,000ft (600m) contour – led to its closure.

b When the track reaches the fence ahead stop and make sure you remember this point for your return. Now turn right, keeping the fence on your left. After you pass the quarry on your right you will eventually come to a stile on your left. Cross it and the ladder stile over the fence which runs in from the left at this point. Continue with the fence on your right and soon the path begins to descend steeply. Take care until you come to the ladder stile at the bottom. Cross it and climb steeply up until you come to Waun Oer. Here you will see a mast set in a rocky knoll to the left of the fence and a trig point to the right of it. On your return be very careful on the descents at the beginning and end of the walk.

The walk is best left for a clear day when the view from Waun Oer is superb. Just south of west is Cadair Idris. This is one of the best views of the range, it being far more picturesque from this angle, when its northern and eastern cwms can be seen, than it is from the north when it appears as a huge (though impressive) wall. North-west are the Rhinogs, beyond the Mawddach, while to the north-east are the Arans. Southward the view is over the green sea of the Dyfi Forest.

To return, reverse the outward route.

Cribin Fawr from the walk

Please note: time taken calculated according to Naismith's Formula (see p.2)

THE ARANS

START/FINISH:
At 853 184, verge parking at the end of the road in Cwm Cywarch. There is no public transport to this point, though there are buses to Dinas Mawddwy about 2½ miles (4km) to the south.

DISTANCE/ASCENT:
10 miles (16km)/2,950ft (900m)

APPROXIMATE TIME:
6 hours

HIGHEST POINT:
2,970ft (905m) Aran Fawddwy

MAPS:
OS Landranger Sheet 124, OS Outdoor Leisure Sheet 23

REFRESHMENTS:
The Red Lion at Dinas Mawddwy is one of the best of Welsh inns. There is also a cafe at the Meirion Mill. There is a Portaloo in an adjacent field with public access

ADVICE:
Boggy in places and with steep drops. Please keep to the footpaths

At 2,970ft (907m) Aran Fawddwy is the highest mountain outside the Snowdon/Glyders/Carneddau area – higher than the more popular Pen y Gadair and tantalisingly close to topping the 3,000ft contour. Sadly the Arans have also been the centre of the longest access dispute in Snowdonia which, together with being a single north-south ridge, has meant it receives fewer visitors than its character and position deserves.

Looking back along Cwm Hengwm from close to the end of the walk

The footpaths on to the Arans are limited and of little value to the walker. This route (and others on the range) follow permissive paths which are indicated (in red) on OS Leisure Sheet 23. These routes are also indicated on notice boards at strategic point near the Arans. The routes are subject to change: please check the notice board before setting out. Please do not leave the permissive paths: access to the Arans is a delicate matter and its continuation is dependent upon the reasonable behaviour of walkers.

A   Cwm Cywarch

Cwm Cywarch is one of Wales secret valleys, overlooked by many who take the mountain road from Dinas Mawddwy to Bala (over Bwlch y Groes). Backed by the impressive cliff of Craig Cywarch – a broken cliff, but one with some good rock climbs – and with good stands of trees, it is a quiet, peaceful valley where the yellow Welsh poppy grows and buzzards circle lazily on updraughts from the cliff. On his Welsh walk in 1854 George Borrow reached Aber Cywarch, the hamlet in the main (Dyfi) valley at the mouth of the cwm finding its 'scenery of the wildest and most picturesque description … there were trees and groves and running waters'. Little, if anything, has changed since Borrow's passing, though it has to be said that part of Borrow's enthusiasm may have stemmed from his mistaking Cwm Cywarch with Glyn Cywarch, near Harlech, and assuming, as a result, that he was close to where the bard Ellis Wynn had written one of his most famous works.

a From the unfenced road end follow the farm road continuation passing a signed path on the right (the return route). Go through the gate along a signed farm track with two ladder stiles. Beyond these bear left on the track to the climbing hut, crossing another ladder stile on the left signed to Rhyd-y-main and Aran, and following a signed path to a footbridge. Beyond the bridge climb the increasingly tight

Aran Fawddwy and Craiglyn Dyfi from Drws Bach

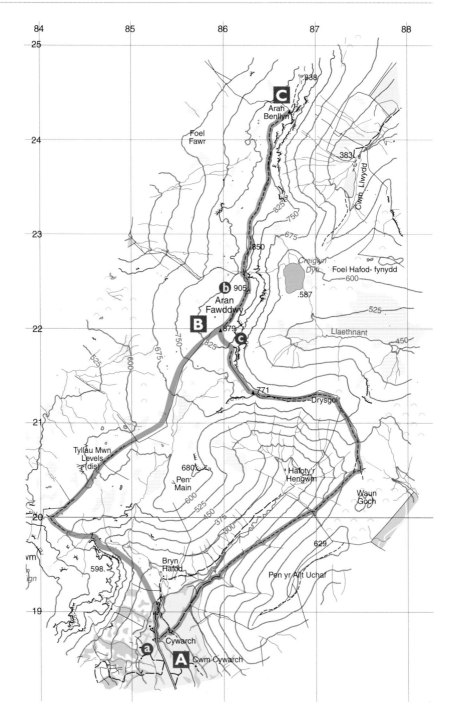

84   85   86   87   88

25

C
838
Aran
Benllyn

24
Foel
Fawr

383
Cwm Llwyd

825
750
675

23
850

Creiglyn
Dyfi
Foel Hafod- fynydd
600
.587

b 905
Aran
Fawddwy
525

B
22
879 ▲
c
825
750
Llaethnant
450

825
675
525   600

771
Drysgol

21
Tyllau Mwn
Levels
(dis)
680
Pen
Main
600
Hafoty'r
Hengwm
Waun
Goch

525
450
375
300

20
629

vm
598.
Bryn
Hafod
Pen yr Allt Uchaf

19
Cywarch

a
A Cwm Cywarch

gorge between Craig Cywarch (left) and Creigiau Camddwr on the right, waymarked by yellow arrows on the rocks, but soon becoming more obvious following a fence on the left.

When the col is reached by a small pool, a path leads off right with white marker posts to reach a fence on the left. Keep ahead with the fence on the left, with long sections of ground planking and ladder stiles over fences to the right. The fence gives the route to the southern summit of Aran Fawddwy. One of the ladder stiles is signed back down to Cwrach – this is the junction of the return path. The further ladder stile is signed to Rhyd-y-main. (Note: the OS map may show this path on the right of the fence.) Climb to the right of the cairn marking the southern top of Aran Fawddwy and then cross the rocky plateau to the actual summit.

B Aran Fawddwy 862 224

The large cairn at the summit was reputedly erected when the locals believed that Pen y Gadair was a few feet higher than their mountain a decision probably, in part at least, due to the number of rich visitors Cadair Idris was attracting. History does not record how the locals felt when they heard they need not have bothered – or when they found that the visitors continued to flock to Cadair.

Nestling below the cliffs of Aran Fawddwy's eastern face is Creiglyn Dyfi, the birthplace of the River Dyfi which vies with the Mawddach for the title of the most beautiful of North Wales' rivers. Further east the col of Bwlch y Groes can be seen, beyond which are the moorland peaks surrounding Lake Vyrnwy. Bwlch y Groes is the Pass of the Cross. Many Welsh passes had crosses erected at their highest points, these being known as 'Thank God' crosses as the traveller could pause on reaching them and thank God that the climbing was over. At Bwlch y Groes a local story maintains that a traveller erected the cross in thanks for his deliverance from a ghostly rider who seemed intent on killing him but who vanished when the traveller made it to the top of the pass.

b

Now continue northwards along the cliff edge, with marvellous views to the east, dropping down to a shallow col, then climbing up to the summit of Aran Benllyn, the summit rocks shining with veins of white quartz.

C Aran Benllyn 866 243

Edmund Spenser's Faerie Queen is an Arthurian romance ignored by most scholars of Arthur's legends because it is a

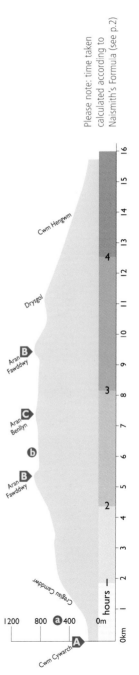

Cwm Cywarch

thinly disguised piece of Tudor propaganda. (In it, Arthur falls in love with Gloriana, the Fairy Queen, who is an even more thinly disguised Queen Elizabeth I.) But one interesting detail of the poem is that it has Arthur educated at the foot of the Arans, and Arthur and Merlin occasionally seeking peace in a cave on the hills. The use of the Arans extends an already long line of stories linking the hills with Arthur. Most famous of these is the battle of Arthur with Rhita Fawr, a giant who lived on the southern edge of Aran Fawddwy. Rhita was a giant who collected beards from men he had killed and stitched them into a cloak to keep out winter's cold. One day Rhita confronted Arthur and some of his knights as they were riding up Bwlch y Groes from Bala. The giant demanded Arthur's beard, saying it would make a fine collar for his cloak. Arthur declined and in the battle which followed killed the giant. The giant's body lay below Aran Fawddwy and Arthur ordered each of his knights to place a stone on it as he passed. this the knights did, the resulting peak being Aran Benllyn.

Rhita Fawr is also claimed to lie below Yr Wyddfa (Snowdon) – see Walk 1 – but it is no longer possible to decide which of the two places has the earliest version of the tale.

c   To return, reverse the route to Aran Fawddwy and on to the cairn marking the southern top. Continue to reach the ladder stile passed on the ascent. Cross the stile and follow the fence on the left to reach Drws Bach, the Little Door, a narrow ridge between the huge amphitheatre of Cwm Hengwm, on the right, and the shallower, but no less picturesque drop of the left. The memorial here is to an RAF man who was killed by lightning in 1960.

Continue beside the fence, following the broadening ridge to Drysgol. The path now turns right (south-east), staying close to a fence as it descends towards a col below Waun Goch. Here a public right of way is reached: bear left and follow the path as it descends into Cwm Hengwm, with magnificent views ahead. The path falls gently, eventually meeting a farm track. Bear left along this, then right along another track which leads to a kissing gate and footbridge, and, soon after, the farm road used on the outward journey. Turn left to return to the start.

Drws Bach and its memorial from Drysgol

ARENIG FAWR

At the eastern edge of the Snowdonia National Park, close to Bala lie the Arenig peaks, towering above a region of wild, wet moorland. This route climbs the highest peak for an incomparable view over a rarely visited area.

A Arenig Fawr

George Borrow, during his journey through Wales in 1854, travelled the road from Ffestiniog to Bala and arrived below Arenig Fawr. He asked a local the peak's name and if anyone lived on it. He was given the name and told that nothing lived on it, neither man nor fox because the peak was too cold. Too cold, the local continued even for a crow, which would starve if it tried to live on the peak. Borrow was impressed by the area's (and the peak's) barrenness and found 'something majestic in its huge bulk. Of all the hills which I saw in Wales none made a greater impression on me'.

It is easy to share Borrow's view. Arenig Fawr is one of the 'Ring of Fire' peaks, the rocky peaks created by igneous intrusions into the Ordovician strata which have created a circle of hard angular mountains. It stands far above the surrounding land, a huge bulk, as Borrow noted, looking like a vast dog crouched ready to pounce on minor irritants such as walkers.

a Cross the stile beside a gate at 846 396 and follow a stony track beyond which climbs to Llyn Arenig Fawr, reaching an old dam/weir and sluice house at its eastern edge.

B Llyn Arenig Fawr

The lake is a claimed site for the legend of the fairy castle, though the story is more usually associated with Llyn Barfog (the Bearded Lake) which lies in the hills of Tarrenhendre on the northern edge of the Dyfi estuary. The legend claims that a local farmer found a young bull calf wandering near the lake and took it home. He reared the animal with care, the calf growing into a magnificent bull which fathered a herd of superb cattle that became the talk of the neighbourhood.

But one day the farmer heard someone calling from the lakeside. To his horror the farmer saw a little old man and realised the man was calling his cows by their names. One by one the cows responded, walking into the lake despite the farmer's attempts to stop them. Too late the farmer realised he had been tricked: the bull calf belonging to the Tylwyth Teg (the little people – the Welsh fairies) who had allowed him to use it to sire a herd from the farmer's cows.

b Go through a gate by the sluice house, over a stream and follow a faint path which climbs the heathery flank of Arenig Fawr, staying close to the edge of the outcrop of Carreg Lefain (at 847 374). The path continues along the edge of Y Castell to reach a fence. Cross the fence and continue climbing on the path to reach a second fence. Just past a corner post cross the fence on your right and follow the path to reach the flatter ground near Bwlch Blaen-y-nant.

There is a faint path bearing left traversing the south-eastern flank of the mountain which soon peters out. To reach the summit you have to strike off to the right at any suitable point. This will involve a stiff climb. When you reach a fence, turn left and follow this up to the remains of a fence (posts). These will lead you to the summit.

An easier, less steep route is not to bear left along the south-eastern flank but to carry on until you reach the fence described above. Turn left and carry on as above.

Arenig Fawr (in the distance) from the south. To the left is Moel Llyfnant

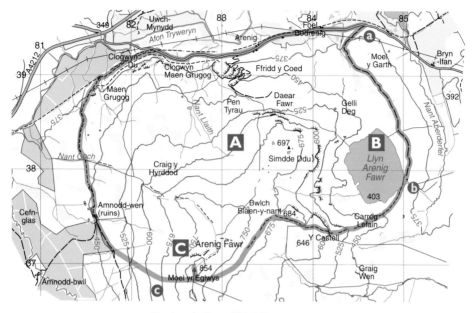

C   Arenig Fawr 828 369

About a century ago the painters Augustus John and James Innes fell, as Borrow had before them, under Arenig Fawr's spell, renting the cottage of Nant Ddu close to the main road (the A4212) to the west of the mountain. Innes, in particularly, had an almost obsessive interest in the peak, seeming to feel an almost spiritual tug from It: he is said to have buried a box of love letters at the summit. Perhaps they lie below the memorial to the American crew of a Flying Fortress which sadly crashed into the mountain on 4 August 1943 with the loss of the entire crew. Arenig Fawr is renowned for its view, but on that day clouds shrouded the peak. The plane almost missed the mountain, hitting just below the summit. The hollow below the memorial to the crew which now crowns the mountain is filled with small pieces of wreckage which are still occasionally found by walkers.

Arenig Fawr's position, towering above the local country, means it is a wonderful viewpoint. To the north, across the main road (the A4212) lies Migneint, 'the quagmire', a vast, trackless, largely featureless, area of moor and marsh which really deserves its occasional title of the last great wilderness in Wales. The area is not inaccessible, an unfenced road (the B4407) defining its northern edge, but its lack of landmarks and reputation for leg-devouring bogs means that those who explore it are likely to be alone with their thoughts and the wind. But in clear weather – it is a harsh place in mist – it is a delight, being nowhere near as wet as claimed and having a variety of interesting bog plants as well as great tracts of heather which are home to a surprising number of birds. The birds (many of which can also be seen on Arenig Fawr) include flocks of curlew, red grouse and snipe, the former with its haunting, rippling cry, the latter two most noticeable when frightened, exploding into the air in a rapid flight. The area is also home to the rare black grouse.

To the south the view extends beyond Llyn Tegid (Bala Lake). The lake is the only place in Britain in which the gwyniad swims. The fish belongs to the salmon family and is believed to have been 'landlocked' when the Ice Ages cut the Afon Dyfrdwy off from the sea. A local legend claims that in the hollow now filled by the lake there once stood the palace of a local chief, a man who ruled the locals with inhuman cruelty and was hated (but feared) by them all. One day the chief threw a party for his cronies and ordered a young harpist to play for them. With reluctance the young man arrived at the palace, not wanting to play for the crowd, but fearing the consequences of not doing so. As he played the revellers became drunk, and what little attention they had paid him ceased. The harpist stopped playing and as he did so a bird landed on his shoulder, whispered 'vengeance' in his ear and flew away. Intrigued, the harpist followed, but each time he reached the bird it whispered 'vengeance' again and flew off. Finally on the hillside, exhausted by the night's playing and by the climb after the bird, the harpist lay down and slept. In the morning, when he looked down into the hollow, Llyn Tegid had been formed, the palace and all the revellers drowned. And floating on the lake was the young man's harp.

c   From the top the most challenging descent returns to the col to the south, then heads north-north-west along a broad ridge, following a fence (and sections of wall) down and across a boggy plateau aiming to reach a track by the forestry. Turn right and follow the waymarked path through the ruins of Amnodd-wen. The path becomes very boggy until you reach a ladder stile. Cross the stile and follow the track until you reach the trackbed of the old GWR railway. Stay on the track (not the trackbed) until you reach the road. Turn right along the road to return to the start.

A shorter and safer descent from the summit is to return by the route you came up.

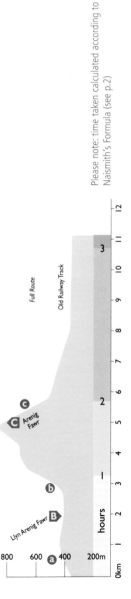

THE BERWYNS

To the north-east of the Arans, and outside the National Park lie the Berwyns, a short ridge of scalloped peaks which are the culmination of a large area of moorland. This route explores the high peaks, starting from Wales highest and most picturesque waterfalls.

A   Pistyll Rhaedr 073 295

Pistyll Rhaedr seems to be one name too many as, translated, it means 'water spout waterfall', but it is really quite appropriate as there are two falls, and the waterfall does indeed start with a spout of water, that shoots out clear of the cliff over which it falls. The total drop is 245ft (75m) making Pistyll Rhaedr the highest in Britain outside the Scottish Highlands. It is also one of the most picturesque, the first, near vertical, fall plunging to a pool beneath a natural arch, from where the water tumbles down a series of cascades. An attempt to cross the arch is definitely not recommended, but there are excellent viewpoints from which the noise and thrash of water can be appreciated.

George Borrow, visiting the falls in 1854 during his journey through Wales (as described in *Wild Wales*) asks 'What shall I liken it to? I scarcely know, unless to an immense skein of silk agitated and disturbed by tempestuous blasts, or to the long tail of a grey courser at furious speed'. It is a very commendable attempt to describe something which is (as Borrow admitted before his trying) almost indescribable. Pistyll Rhaedr must be seen and heard, its power experienced rather than being described. The falls are very young (on a geological timescale) having been formed about 10,000 years ago by the glaciation of the last Ice Age. The vertical drop of the top section of the falls reflects their youth: in time the Afon Disgynfa will cut back its head and smooth the drop.

The stream below the falls is home to dippers, while the trees and hedges close by harbour a variety of species including nuthatches, tree creepers, pied flycatchers, redstarts and green woodpeckers.

a   Take the signposted footpath through a gate just at the entrance of the car park, going through further gates to reach a stony track above a stream (to the right). When this track bends sharply and steeply to the left cross over the stream and go through the gate on the opposite side. Follow this path uphill to another path junction. Turn left and follow this path to its end, where it reaches the Nant y Llyn stream (the outflow of Llyn Lluncaws) at 076 310.

After you have crossed this second stream make your way along the path to the southern end of Llyn Lluncaws. Bear left (west) taking the path climbing the ridge to the top of Moel Sych.

B The Berwyns

The high Berwyn peaks, forming a ridge that runs almost due north-south, were a barrier to ice flowing eastwards from Snowdonia, causing local glaciers which plucked at the high ridge as they tumbled over it, then carved deep hollows at the base of the cliffs it created. The result was the series of impressively steep cwms along the eastern edge of the high peaks. The surprise is that there is only one lake in the glacial hollows – Llyn Lluncaws below Moel Sych. The cwms below Cadair Berwyn and Cadair Bronwen were not sufficiently over-deepened for glacial moraine to create dams, though below Cadair Berwyn the cwm is very boggy.

Pistyll Rhaedr and the start of the walk from the path to the Berwyns

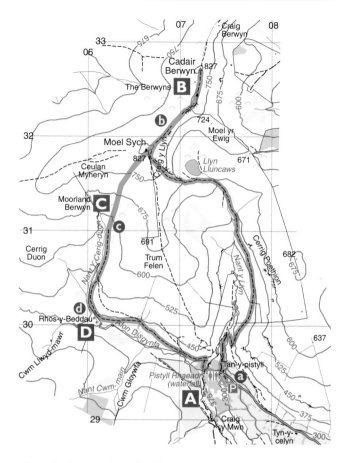

Moel Sych (the Dry Peak) was the highest peak in old Montgomeryshire. It now stands at the border of Powys and Clwyd: the other high peaks all stand in the latter county.

b Now follow the high Berwyn ridge to Cadair Berwyn. The walk can be continued to Cadair Bronwen, adding about 3 miles (5km) for the round trip. As Cadair Bronwen is the northern extremity of the Berwyn ridge the views north towards the Dee Valley are tremendous. Cadair Bronwen is also a 2,572ft peak (784m) and therefore a significant prize.

To return, regain the summit of Moel Sych and take the permissive footpath signposted Pystill Rhaeadr for a short distance. Before the first steep descent you reach three half-buried stones, pick up the faint path going off to the right. This permissive path is difficult to follow. It takes you across a short piece of very rough ground to Cwm Rhiawiau. It is worth persevering as this is a very attractive hidden valley.

C Moorland Berwyn

Moorland Berwyn is heather – thick, deep heather which makes an exploration of the moor a feat of willpower – alternating with damp patches of sphagnum moss and interspersed with several varieties of berries, including crowberry, cowberry and cranberry. The very lucky will also spot cloudberry, the moor being one of the very few places the plant thrives south of Hadrian's Wall. So rare, but prized was the cloudberry that any local presenting the local vicar with a quart of them was excused all church tithes for a year. Almost as rare is the lesser twayblade, an orchid despite the name, a short plant with large oval leaves and a tiny, greenish-red flower. The moor is also home to several rare birds, particularly the hen harrier, merlin, short-eared owl and golden plover. There are also red and black grouse, the moor being managed – by the lighting of small scale fires to clear old heather and so encourage new growth – for the benefit of these birds. The Welsh grouse population has fallen and an increase in numbers will benefit the raptors.

The moor is also famous for its bad weather: in August 1165 Henry II's army was caught out on it by a tremendous storm. As one of the army noted, it was 'a mighty tempest of wind and exceeding great torrents of rain'. After a few days of being soaked and numbingly cold the king was so outraged by the weather that he had all the Welsh prisoners taken on the campaign blinded. It seems Henry was convinced that the

The Berwyns from the southern end of the valley of the Nant y Llyn. In the centre of the far ridge is Cadair Berwyn with Moel Sych to the left

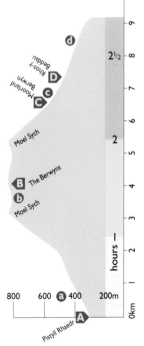

Please note: time taken calculated according to Naismith's Formula (see p.2)

Pistyll Rhaedr

Welsh had somehow conjured up the weather – those who fought against Owain Glyndwr were also convinced that he could whistle up a winter's storm in mid-summer – but the Berwyns have always been known for their ability to engineer such weather. The cold wind that often sweeps the moor is known local as Gwynt Traed y Meirw – the Wind from the Feet of the Dead. Appropriately the Berwyns are another area believed to be hunted by Gwyn ap Nudd and the Hounds of the Underworld (see Note to Walk 23). To the west of the high ridge the upland is known as Carnedd y Ci, the Hill of the Dogs, as this was the main area of Gwyn's sweep across the moors.

c Follow the stream south to its confluence with a smaller stream coming in from the right. To the west of this confluence, on a section of flat land, are a series of standing stones, half hidden among the heather.

D Rhos-y-Beddau 059 302

Presumably in Bronze Age times the moor was a little more hospitable as there are a number of burials and megalithic sites, particularly on the moorland close to Pistyll Rhaedr. At Rhos-y-Beddau there is a stone circle and a 200ft (60m) row of standing stones.

d From the stone circle a faint path leads to a gate by the stream. Go through and follow a more distinct path beside the stream. Soon the roar of water falling over Pistyll Rhaedr can be heard: a marker post points the way to a viewpoint near the top (though the view is not as good as that from the bottom as the sheer drop precludes a proper look down the falls). The main path continues eastwards: soon, at another marker post, bear right to reach the bottom of the falls.

Looking back to Moel Sych from a cairn on the moorland to the south

28

YR EIFL

START/FINISH:
The car park at 353 441, about ¾ mile (1km) to the north of Llithfaen. Llithfaen is on a bus route from Trefor to Tudweiliog (connecting with a service from Pwllheli to Penygroes) and is also the terminus for a bus from Pwllheli

DISTANCE/ASCENT:
5 miles (8km)/1,400ft (425m)

APPROXIMATE TIME:
3½ hours

HIGHEST POINT:
1,850ft (564m) Yr Eifl

MAPS:
OS Landranger Sheet 123, OS Explorer Sheet 254

REFRESHMENTS:
Limited selection in Llithfaen, rather better in Llanaelhaearn

ADVICE:
A moderately strenuous, historically interesting walk with terrific views. Ensure that this walk is attempted on a clear day

On the Llyn Peninsula, within view of the Snowdonia peaks, but often free of their cloud, lie the Rivals, a small range of hills formed by the same processes that created the high Snowdon peaks. This walk explores the range, offering a superb viewpoint on clear days.

A   Nant Gwrtheyrn
It is said that Vortigern, a Celtic leader living in Kent after the departure of the Romans in the 5th century AD, was in danger of losing a war with a neighbouring tribe and decided to hire mercenaries to bolster his own troops. Vortigern brought Saxons across the water from Europe: they were excellent fighters and Vortigern won his war. But the Saxons liked Kent and declined to go home. Instead they brought across their families and invited their friends. They set up villages and, enthusiastic about their new land, pushed their Celtic neighbours westward to create more space. Historians believe this story of the first Saxon 'invasion' of Britain to be simplistic, but concede that there may be an element of truth in it.

The legend of Vortigern continues beyond the first settlement of Kent by the Saxons. It maintains that, appalled by his stupidity his tribe banished him from his former kingdom. Other Celts, seeing the likely future only too clearly, also chased him away and he was forced to seek refuge in the mountains of Snowdonia. At first he settled on Dinas Emrys

Yr Eifl from the start of the walk

where his story mingles with that of Merlin (see Note to Walk 15) but eventually he moved to a remote, secret valley on the lonely Lleyn Peninsula. The valley is still known as Vortigern's Valley (in Welsh Nant Gwrtheyrn). The legend maintains that Vortigern died here and in the 17th century a large mound, believed to be the king's castle, was demolished by amateur archaeologists/treasure hunters. At its base they found the skeleton of a man in a stone coffin who, they assumed, was the king. Nothing now remains of the site, but historians believe that the diggers had probably been working on a long barrow. Nant Gwrtheyrn lies a short distance to the north of the start point of this walk and can be seen clearly from the walk's early stages.

Looking towards Tre'r Ceiri from the high summit of Yr Eifl

a From the car park, turn right but very soon go sharp left along a bridleway, following it uphill to the pass of Bwlch yr Eifl, between the range's northern and central peaks. From this bridleway there is a superb view of Vortigern's Valley, to the left. Just beyond the top of the pass – opposite a gated vehicle track, left, leading to a mast – turn right along a path which climbs steadily uphill to the highest of the Rival peaks, marked by a large cairn, an old shelter and a trig. point.

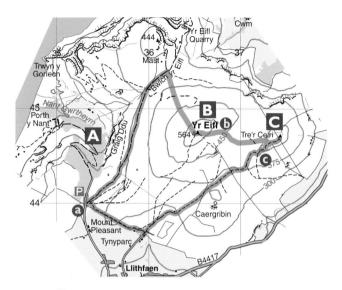

B   Yr Eifl 365 447

The peak is the central prong of the fork – Yr Eifl in Welsh – of three peaks at the northern edge of the Lleyn Peninsula. It is the Welsh name, or rather its pronunciation – Ear Ivel – which gave the peaks their English name, Rivals. From the peak the view of the Snowdonia peaks is superb. One is almost tempted to say unrivalled.

b   Leave the summit in an easterly direction by a path going directly towards the next summit (Tre'r Ceiri). After about 100 yards (90m) a cairn of stones is reached where the path divides. Go sharp left, at first along the contour of the hill, and then dropping down, still aiming at the summit of Tre'r Ceiri. Soon you are able to see the track through the heather in the col below, leading up to a gap in the outer wall of the ancient settlement ahead. Go through the gap and then right along a path going up to a gap in the inner wall. Once through this gap, go left up to the summit.

C   Tre'r Ceiri

Tre'r Ceiri means the Town of Giants, and it is easy to see why local folk, reaching the site centuries after it had been abandoned, might well have believed that it had been built by superhumans. Even now it is not clear who built the settlement – though modern historians lean more towards late Celtic or Romano-British builders than to giants. It is likely that there were actually two phases of occupation/building, the first pre-dating the Romans, the second during the Roman occupation. The amount of excavated Roman pottery favours the latter as the main period of settlement. The site is large (though not huge), an oval of long axis 300m (1,000 ft) and short axis 100m (330ft), surrounded by a stone wall up to 15ft (4.5m) thick and including a walkway for guards. Though the use of stone rather than earth and wooden fencing is more sophisticated than the usual Celtic (Iron Age) hill fort, the site's defences conforms to the normal pattern. But inside those defences it most certainly does not conform to the norm. Here lie the

Looking south-west along the Lleyn Peninsula from the high summit of Yr Eifl

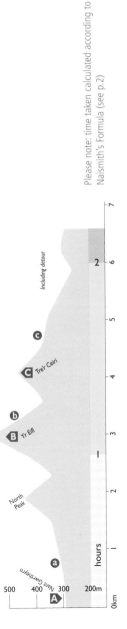

Please note: time taken calculated according to Naismith's Formula (see p.2)

Looking north-west to Bwlch yr Eifl and the westernmost Rivals peak from the high summit of Yr Eifl

remains of over 150 huts, many of them the 'standard' Iron Age circular pattern, but some a curious egg shape. Even more intriguingly there are also huts outside the walls, and these were built on raised platforms, constructed to level the building base, hardly a temporary arrangement it might be argued.

Normally hillforts were used by folk retreating from a threat, either a land-borne army or – and more likely given the position of the Rivals – sea-borne pirates. Once inside the fort they would sit out a siege: sieges were always short, no leader could maintain a sizeable army in the field for long at that time. But here the huts imply a more sustained occupation. But quite who the hut dwellers were, or what they did for a living is a mystery.

In the early 19th century a local woman claimed to have been told in a dream that a vast treasure in gold lay buried at the site. She mentioned her dream the next day and within hours the site had been invaded by an army of men carrying shovels and picks. Archaeologists have despaired over the digging the men carried out, and the work of those gold-diggers (literally!) means that today's casual visitor has difficulty picking out the remains of many huts.

Below the hill top, to the east, is the village of Llanaelhaearn, once an important pilgrimage stop on the way to Bardsey Island off the Lleyn's western tip. Bardsey (named, it is believed, for a Viking warrior: in Welsh the island is Ynys

Enlli) was the site of the first monastery in Wales and was said to be the burial ground of 20,000 Celtic saints. Three pilgrimages to Bardsey were the equal to one to Rome on the medieval scale of indulgences. The island was said to be so sacred that no one who lived on it would ever die of disease, only of old age. This must have been very comforting to everyone except the eldest inhabitant.

c   Leave Tre'r Ceiri by the same gaps in the inner and outer walls. One outside (by an information board) go left along a narrow path. When a broad track is reached go right along it, but in about 100 yards (90m) leave this track to take a narrower path half right. This reaches a wall at a gate and ladder stile. Cross the stile and proceed ahead to another ladder stile. Cross it and take the path going half left down to a covered water tank. Go past the tank and turn right along a wide track leading towards a house. About 200 yards (180m) before the house bear right to reach a wall. At the wall go right along a track which goes back to the road near the starting point.

The high summit of Yr Eifl

NEWBOROUGH WARREN

🛈 ✏ 🌿 🍂 🍃 🌳

START/FINISH:
The car park at 411 671, just off the A4080 to the north-west of Newborough. Newborough (Niwbwrch) is on the route of buses from Bangor to Llangefni, and has its own bus route to Llangefni. The walk can be significantly reduced in length if the car park (fee payable) at 406 634 is used, but this misses the views across Malltraeth

DISTANCE/ASCENT:
8½ miles (13km) (3½ miles/ 6km) if Warren car park is used)/120ft (35m)

APPROXIMATE TIME:
4 hours

MAPS:
OS Landranger Sheet 114, OS Pathfinder Sheet 768 (OS Explorer Sheet 263)

REFRESHMENTS:
Available in Newborough, but bringing a picnic is recommended

ADVICE:
An easy forest and shoreline walk. Llanddwyn is an island for a few hours each side of high tide, so be cautious if crossing to it on a rising tide. Dogs are not allowed on Llanddwyn Island

O ften, when it is wet in the National Park, the Snowdonia mountains shrouded in cloud, it is dry just across the Menai Straits on Anglesey. This walk explores one of the island's most interesting areas, the dunes that lie within sight of Caernarfon.

A Newborough

The kings of Gwynedd knew the value of the island of Anglesey to the security of their land. The mountains of Snowdonia and their fearsome weather might be a barrier against invading armies, but it was Anglesey, Mam Cymru (the Mother of Wales) that was the kingdom's granary. Safe behind the mountain wall, and beyond the tidal race which ripped through the Menai Straits (the current can reach 8 knots, was a hazard to even the most experienced ferrymen and often lethal to the inexperienced), Gwynedd's lords could wait, well-fed, for invaders to become disillusioned. Small wonder that one of the main palaces of the kings was on the island, at Aberffraw.

In 1295 Edward I, realising the importance of the island, decided to build the eighth and last castle of his 'Ring of Stone' castles close to the island's western tip, overlooking the Menai Straits, but remote from its narrow, deadly section. The land chosen was a pleasant section of marshland, a *beau marais* in courtly French: Beaumaris in our modern tongue. But close to the chosen site was a Welsh village. Not wanting possible

In Newborough Forest close to the start of the walk

The Snowdonian peaks from Llanddwyn Island

rebels living quite so close the Welsh were evicted, their village destroyed. The families were given a 'new borough' at the other end of the Menai Straits. The new site was a bleak, inhospitable piece of windswept scrub, and in case there were those in the old village who did not favour the move Edward offered a financial inducement – move or be fined.

Today Newborough is a pleasant place with a fine, 19th century clock tower. Anciently the villagers made a living by harvesting the marram grass from the dunes and weaving it into mats, baskets and ropes, though this trade has now largely disappeared. The church – dedicated to St Peter – on the road towards the sea dates from the early 14th century, having been built soon after the founding of the village. Inside there are tomb slabs dating from the 14th century, but the font is perhaps two centuries earlier: did it come from the villagers' original church? With its intricate carving it is a fine piece of work.

a With your back to the road, take the left-hand path out of the car park which leads to a forest track after about 110 yards (100m). Turn right on the track. When you have passed a bird hide on stilts take the first track to the right (FP17). Follow this track which has views across the village and the Bodorgan Headland. (FPs are numbered forest posts.)

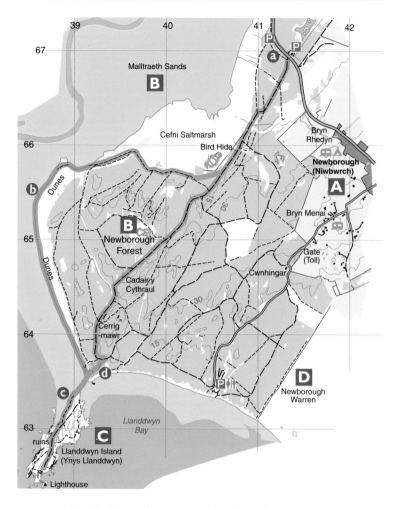

B Newborough Forest/Malltraeth Sands

Crossbills live in the forest, though it is more likely that they
will be heard – a metallic 'kip, kip' – than seen. Out on the
estuary there are numerous wildfowl and waders (especially
redshank, and greenshank in winter) but the main interest is
the migratory species, which can include avocets. Malltraeth
was the home of the wildlife artist Charles Tunnicliffe for the
last 30 years of his life.

b Follow the track as it crosses the mud flats at the edge of
the estuary. On very high spring tides these can be flooded
and it will be necessary to cross the rougher ground close to
the forest edge. Be careful of the tides on this section.

When the track reaches the sand dunes after 2 miles (3.2km), bear right on to the beach and cross the sandy headland of Traeth Penrhos, heading towards the now visible Llanddwyn Island, with an expanding view of the Lleyn Peninsula. Where the island joins the beach, look out for the pillow lava – formations which look like pillows, caused by the lava being extruded underwater. This makes the island a favourite with geologists.

C   Llanddwyn Island

Llanddwyn is an island only at high tide. It is part of the Newborough Warren Nature Reserve and so walker's should keep to the track across it: the track visits the island's major points of interest. In the 5th century the island was the hermitage home of the female Celtic St Dwynwen. It is said that St Dwynwen came to the island to escape the memory of an unhappy love affair, the legend claiming that in order to avoid temptation she prayed that she and her lover be made impotent. A potion miraculously appeared: it had the desired effect on St Dwynwen, but turned her lover into a block of ice. Was this the ultimate symbol of frigidity?

As one who had suffered in love, St Dwynwen achieved a reputation for offering advice on matters of the heart. Locals, and others from all over Anglesey and Snowdonia, would visit the island and sprinkle breadcrumbs on the waters of the well St Dwynwen drank from (and which still stands beside the old church). A handkerchief was then spread over the crumbs. The well was said to be home to an eel placed there by the saint. When the eel rose to eat the breadcrumbs, if the handkerchief was undisturbed then the relationship the crumb sprinkler was questioning would turn out well, but if the handkerchief was disturbed then the questioner's lover would be unfaithful.

Following St Dwynwen's occupation the island acquired such a reputation for sanctity that a monastery was built on the hermitage site in the late 15th/early 16th century. When Henry VIII dissolved it, as he dissolved all monastic houses following his break with Rome, Llanddwyn was the richest monastery in Snowdonia. Use of the ruin as an easy quarry for building stone, and centuries of wind, rain and frost then ravaged the island: today only sections of the chancel walls remains. The Celtic cross is modern, erected over the place where human bones (probably those of medieval monks) were uncovered during excavations. The Latin cross commemorates St Dwynwen.

Please note: time taken calculated according to Naismith's Formula (see p.2)

13
2½ 12
11
2 10
9
8
c
7
C
Llanddwyn Island
6
b
5
4
B
3
Newborough Forest & Malltraeth Sands
2
hours
1
a
50   0m
0km

c   If the tide is right, follow the well-defined footpath across the island to reach the information centre in the old pilot's cottage at the far end. After exploring the island, reverse the route along the footpath, passing to the left (west) of the pillow lava to reach the beach. To explore the dunes of Newborough Warren – a more extensive dune system than that crossed on the route, with a better developed group of habitats – turn right and walk along the beach. Beyond the forest edge is the dune system. The path around the island is good for views and also visits all points of interest; this will add 3 miles (5km) to the walk.

D   Newborough Warren

The Warren is the sixth largest dune site in Britain. At the time of the setting up of the new village it is thought to have been smaller, but the transplanted Welsh folk, anxious to find fertile land to farm near their new homes, cut and burned the scrub covering the land to the south. In a very short time the wind had buried the newly exposed land with sand. Such a problem was the growing area of dunes that marram grass was planted to stabilise the sand. In Elizabethan times a law was passed forbidding the cutting of the grass, although, as noted above, the villagers were eventually able to harvest the grass. The villagers also introduced rabbits – thus adding the name 'warren' to their 'new borough' – and successfully

The renovated pilots' cottages on Llanddwyn Island

harvested the animals for food and fur. The warren yielded between 80,000 and 100,000 rabbits annually for centuries, an astonishing number. Only with the outbreak of myxomatosis in 1954 did the harvesting stop, the disease virtually wiping out the rabbit population.

The dunes, the adjacent salt marshes and Llanddwyn Island now form a Nature Reserve. The dunes show a succession from new (plant-free, friable sand) to old (compacted sand with a variety of plants), and also have a remarkable number of microsystems – it is not just a boring succession of dunes, there are wetter areas (in the 'slacks' – hollows – between the dunes), and also shady and sunlight spots, each having its unique flora and fauna. Close to the sea the visitor will find sea rocket, with its pale lilac flowers, sea sandwort and spear-leafed orache, while further back are sea couch grass and lyme grass. The highest dunes are held together by marram, but are also home to the elegant, but prickly, sea holly, common ragwort and common catsear. Behind the tallest dunes grow mouse-ear hawkweed (like a small, pale dandelion), carline thistle, lady's bedstraw and wild pansy. In the slacks the walker may find creeping willow and the delicate marsh pennywort. Rarest of all are plants of *Epipactis dunensis*, the dune helleborine, a very rare variant of the narrow-lipped helleborine.

The remains of a wooden boat on Traeth Penrhos. In the distance the Snowdonian peaks frame Llanddwyn Island

The bird life includes oyster catchers and lapwings, meadow pipits and the increasingly rare skylark. The once (relatively) common short-eared owls and Montagu's harrier can still be seen occasionally, but numbers have sadly declined. The salt marshes are home to flocks of waders, while the islets off Llanddwyn Island hold breeding colonies of shags and cormorants. But easiest of all to spot is the herring gull. The dunes are home to vast numbers of snails, many with very colourful (and beautiful) shells, and the herring gulls, one of nature's best examples of an opportunistic feeder, have found them to their taste. At the tide line, walkers will find other shells – razor shells and oysters to name but two – among the seaweed and detritus.

d Coming off the island, turn left back onto the beach you came down, and immediately take the path between the dunes and the rocks which leads back to a forest track (110 yards/100m), turn right on this track. In 65 yards (50m), at the next track (FP6) turn left and follow this back to join the same track you set out on (FP17) and then make your way back to the car park.

GREAT ORME

START/FINISH:
Gloddaeth Road, Llandudno. Parking is easy at its western end, There are also car parks in the town and several on Great Orme itself

DISTANCE/ASCENT:
5½ miles (9km)/650ft (200m)

APPROXIMATE TIME:
2½ hours

HIGHEST POINT:
590ft (180m) on the northern slopes of Great Orme

MAPS:
OS Landranger Sheet 115, OS Outdoor leisure Sheet 17

REFRESHMENTS:
Possibilities almost without number in Llandudno, from kiosk to grand restaurant. There are also picnic sites on Great Orme and a cafe at the ski centre

ADVICE:
A very easy walk with much of interest and fine views – take care on the cliffs

The final 'rain-shadow' walk heads east from the main Snowdonian peaks, visiting a limestone headland thrust out into the sea from the Victorian seaside resort of Llandudno.

A   Llandudno

The resort of Llandudno began in the 1840 and rapidly rose to one of the most popular on the north Wales coast, its popularity helped by its having two bays, one facing north (North Shore) and one facing Conwy (West Shore). The Victorian popularity of the town is reflected in its array of fine buildings. One of the many famous visitors from that period was Charles Lutwidge Dodgson (Lewis Carroll) who is said to have drawn inspiration for *Alice in Wonderland* from trips he made to the local dunes in the company of Alice Liddell the young daughter of the Dean of his college (Dodgson was a mathematics lecturer at Oxford) with whom he stayed. The White Rabbit Memorial on the West Shore is a reminder of Llandudno's part in the creation of the book.

From Llandudno a tramway was built in 1902 to take visitors up on to the Great Orme. It is still functioning and has several claims to fame, being the longest cable driven tramway in Britain and one of only three funicular trams in the world.

a   From the end of Gloddaeth Avenue, follow the road towards Great Orme, soon passing the road's toll house (the road which circumnavigates Great Orme is a toll road for vehicles). Behind the tollhouse there is a path running parallel to the road. However, the road is a good alternative as it allows a fine view of the Conwy estuary which the path (being behind houses) misses. The footpath rejoins the road after about 1,000 yards (900m): continue along the road, but take the next path on the right, following it uphill to reach a T-junction.

B   Great Orme

It is thought that the headland's name derives from the Viking word for a sea monster. But not because the headland was a popular place for spotting such mythical beats, rather because in profile it looks like the monsters of legend: the more so perhaps if it reared up out of the mist to confront approaching ships.

The headland's rock could hardly be a greater contrast to the hard, igneous rocks of Snowdon, being limestone, a sedimentary rock laid down below a calm sea rather than ejected by explosive volcanic action. The rock comprises the shells and skeletons of sea creatures of the Carboniferous era and interested walkers will find fossil crinoids and bivalves without too much effort.

Llandudno Pier and Little Orme from near the Ski Centre

The soil formed by the head's limestone supports plants which are as different from those of Snowdonia as is the landscape. The ice sheets of the last Ice Age removed all, or most, of any existing soil, the present surface being a mix of bare rock and a thin, lime-rich soil in which grows a very specific range of plants. Of the plants that need a reasonable depth of soil the most common are salad burnet, common and hoary rock-rose

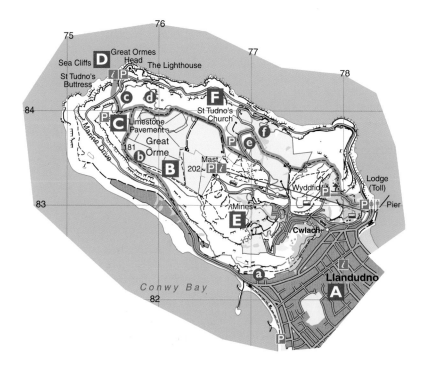

and the beautiful, pale lilac harebell. Patches of even deeper soil support heather and gorse and flowers such as tormentil and the delicate, lilac flowered heath speedwell. In the thinner soil found in the cracks of the barer rocks several unusual ferns – including black spleenwort – thrive, as does dog's mercury.

Of the rarer species of plant on the Orme, now mostly confined to the steep cliffs where the sheep and feral goats cannot graze, patient walkers might find common scurvy grass – the Vitamin C rich plant that was the ancient cure for scurvy – sea campion, and the beautiful, crimson-coloured bloody cranesbill. The goats that graze the shallower cliffs are the descendants of Windsor Park's royal herd of Kashmir goats released on to headland in about 1900. With their creamy coats and large horns they are the most impressive of the headland's wildlife.

The great variety of wildflowers and the mild climate of the headland (relatively to the mountains at least) mean that Great Orme is famous for its butterflies. Indeed, the headland is of national importance for its butterfly population. Of the rarer species the lucky walker may see the sub-species of the silver-studded blue (a slightly smaller butterfly than the usual form) and the grayling (which feeds on common rock-rose) each of which is unique to Great Orme. Of other unusual species the most spectacular is the dark-green fritillary.

b Turn left and follow a well-defined path which heads north-west, then turns west to reach an area of limestone pavement.

C Limestone Pavement 757 839

Not only is the rock different from that of the high Snowdonian peaks, but its form is also different. While the high peaks were moulded by the glaciers which flowed down their slopes, the Orme's flat limestone sheet was merely scoured clean, creating a vast, almost flat rock sheet – the plateau that we now see. The limestone is not a uniform rock, and differential erosion of the exposed surface, chiefly by rainwater, has created a pattern of deep cracks separating areas of more resistant rock. The cracks are known as grykes, the less weathered areas clints. Though the Great Orme's clints and grykes are not as extensive as those of the huge limestone pavements of the Yorkshire Dales, they are a very good example of the form. They are also very good at tripping the unwary so please take care.

c The path has joined a wall near the pavement: continue beside the wall to where it turns abruptly right. From here a detour to the left soon reaches a view over the high cliffs near Great Ormes Head

D Sea Cliffs

The cliffs are home to a variety of sea birds, including razorbills, guillemots and kittiwakes, as well as the much rarer chough. Interestingly the cliffs also support a small population of little owls. Inland, the headland is home to whinchats, stonechats and wheatears, and to meadow pipits whose mating flight, a helicoptering descent, enlivens any springtime walk. In winter the lucky walker may see snow buntings on the headland and red-throated divers on the sea.

d When the wall goes right, turn with it, following the path as it heads east. The path becomes a gravel track and, soon after, reaches a road. To reach the summit of the headland, turn right here, then right again at a T-junction.

E Great Orme Mines

Copper has been worked on Great Orme since Bronze Age

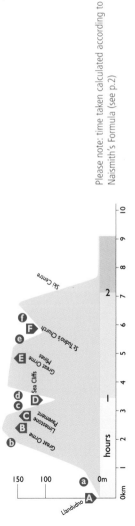

Please note: time taken calculated according to Naismith's Formula (see p.2)

The path between St Tudno's Church and the Ski Centre

times (about 3,500 years ago), although the headland was inhabited even earlier, Palaeolithic (Old Stone Age) remains having been found in Kendricks Cave on the southern flank. It is assumed that the Romans worked the ore, though there is no direct evidence, but the headland was then left to farmers until the 17th century when the copper was again worked. The original workings had been surface (ie. open cast) but as these deposits were exhausted adits (horizontal shafts) were driven. The mines are now open to the public and include both Palaeolithic and Bronze Age artefacts discovered on the headland.

e   Turn left and follow the road to St Tudno's Church.

F   St Tudno's Church 769 838

Tudno was a 6th century Celtic saint who set up his llan – religious site, either a hermit's cell or a small settlement for the saint and his disciples – on the headland. The town of Llandudno is named for the saint's llan. Tudno's first church was probably built of wood, but there was certainly a stone church on this site by the 12th century. That church was enlarged in the 15th century, but then neglected. In the early 19th century a storm blew the roof off, leaving it a decaying ruin. However in 1855 a full restoration was carried out.

f Follow the road past the church, but then turn right along a footpath signed for Llandudno and the Ski Centre. Follow this path, forking left after 270 yards (250m), to reach a farm. Here take the path signed for the Ski Centre climbing around the flank of Mynydd Isaf. From here, on clear days, there are views of the Lake District and Blackpool Tower, and more local ones along the north Wales coast.

When a fork is reached – there is a tremendous view over Llandudno from close to here – bear left, down steps, and walk through the Happy Valley park, with the Ski Centre on your left. The Centre has a toboggan run as well as a standard ski slope. When the path reaches a road, bear left, following the road to reach a main road in Llandudno close to the pier. Follow this road (the Promenade) around a section of the North Shore, then bear right along the main road. This is Gloddaeth Street: follow it back to the start. Alternatively, there is a good path through Haulfre Gardens and along the invalid's walk, leading to Abbey Road or the toll house.

St Tudno's Church

COLLINS *rambler's guide*

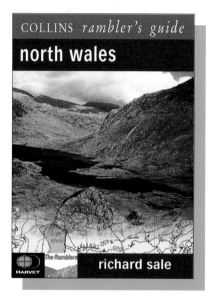

COLLINS *rambler's guide*

north wales

richard sale

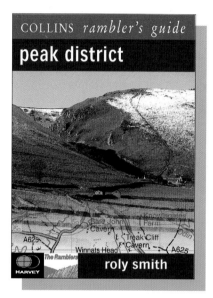

COLLINS *rambler's guide*

peak district

roly smith

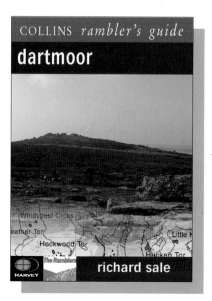

COLLINS *rambler's guide*

dartmoor

richard sale

COLLINS *rambler's guide*

ben nevis & glen coe

chris townsend